The Push Hands Workbook:

T'ai Chi partner movements (Tui Shou) for sport and personal development

Nando Raynolds

Raynolds, Nando, 1960 –
The push hands workbook.

Includes bibliographical references.
Push hands. 2. T'ai Chi. 3. Martial Arts.
4. Relationships. 5. Title.

With special thanks to Brian Thoroman, Karin Burroughs for her photography, Debby Thornton for her studio, my kind reviewers. my teachers and my many students for their years of input into my own learning.

May this book contribute to the understanding
and development of Push Hands.

Table of Contents:

Push hands workbook study guide:

Put the date on the line to keep track of your progress and what you still have to practice.

	Still have to think about it	Proficient
Chapter 3 - Drills and Games Level 1		
Sticking	_____	_____
Weight shifting	_____	_____
Wrist and elbow joint circling	_____	_____
Sticking with wrists	_____	_____
Twisting around center	_____	_____
Neutralizing	_____	_____
Finding your root w/standing	_____	_____
Immoveable ward off	_____	_____
Free form game 1 – Seeking Center	_____	_____
Chapter 4 - Understanding the process of pushing		
Perceiving your partner's center	_____	_____
Understanding double weighting	_____	_____
Understanding vectors	_____	_____
The error of force against force	_____	_____
The error of leaning	_____	_____
Chapter 5 - Drills and Games Level 2		
Listening to the push	_____	_____
Single hand circling	_____	_____
Closing the forward kua	_____	_____
Solo Pushing	_____	_____
Pushing with a partner	_____	_____
Uprooting	_____	_____
Correcting your partner's errors by striking	_____	_____
Snake arms	_____	_____
Free form game 2: fixed step free push hands	_____	_____
Chapter 6 – Higher level internal skills		
Yi or attention/intent	_____	_____
Mental toughness	_____	_____
Sneaky energy manipulations	_____	_____

About Nando Raynolds:

I was lucky enough to enroll in a T'ai Chi class in 1978 and have been practicing ever since. My practice has been an extremely valuable constant in my life. I have had the privilege of studying with a number of fine teachers over the years, most from the Cheng Man Ch'ing (CMC) Yang style. My teachers have included Paul Gallagher, Susan De Foe, Ben Lo, Lenzie Williams, Jane and Bataan Faigao, Chris Luth, George Xu and Sam Masich. I have been teaching privately and at the college level since 1988. My training has been less formal than is ideal due to my penchant for moving when I was younger and then living these last 18 years in a small community in Southern Oregon.

Since 1992 I have also studied Shotokan and Kenpo Karate with Thomas Spellman and hold my second degree black belt in Daimon Ryu. Since the 5th grade, I have been doing recreational yoga. In 1986, I started doing massage professionally and have taught massage at the local massage school. My bodywork background includes an understanding of Alexander Technique, Feldenkrais and postural deep tissue work. I mention these because the perspective I bring to T'ai Chi is colored by these studies.

In my experience there are four kinds of T'ai Chi players. The most common is the person who studies for a while, even a few years, and then gets distracted or goes on to something else. The second type makes a more serious and long-term commitment to T'ai Chi including daily practice and ongoing classes or seminars. The third is the rare person for whom the study of T'ai Chi and the internal arts becomes their life focus, including regular multi-hour practice and connection with recognized masters. The fourth, and most precious, are those who have studied T'ai Chi and other martial arts six or more hours a day for decades.

I am a serious student of T'ai Chi of the second type. I am frequently made aware of how much more I have to learn, but I have never been called to devote my life to this study. My primary work now is as a psychotherapist for adults and couples. I am a good teacher and a clear communicator, but, unfortunately, not an enlightened Taoist sage or T'ai Chi Master. Nonetheless, my hope is that this book will help make the process of learning push hands skills more straightforward for you.

It is often said in the martial arts that the primary opponent is ourselves. This refers to the challenge of disciplining yourself to do a little "bitter" practice each day, and to overcoming your character defects. I am most interested in helping my students have happy lives and helping them build their character. Push hands, if done as a training method (as opposed to a contest), is an incomparable tool for confronting fear, anger, pride and selfishness, and for cultivating kindness, compassion, humility and presence. May it serve you in this way.

I wrote the practical portion of The Everything Book on T'ai Chi and Qigong, and have produced several video and dvd programs on T'ai Chi, Qigong and Energy Medicine. Visit my website at www.nando-r.com to find out more. I welcome seminar inquiries.

I'm going to let my push hands partner for this text introduce himself:

About Brian Thoroman

I have been studying Cheng Man Ch'ing Yang Style T'ai Chi with Nando Raynolds since 1997 and have been lucky enough to often work privately with him during that time exploring both the form and push hands. Nando certified me as a junior instructor in 2003 and I have had the pleasure of sharing T'ai Chi with a variety of individuals and groups in both Flagstaff, AZ and Ashland, OR.

I have also studied Chen Style Lao Jia and Chi Kung with Dr. Yung-Sen Chen, as well as practiced many styles of Yoga and Chi Kung. Many fellow students and teachers have generously tossed me about over the years and often added pearls of wisdom to my training in the process. As a massage therapist and personal trainer, I have a dedicated desire to more deeply understand the body in movement and health. My personal practice is the cornerstone of the quality of my health, work and relationships.

I am extremely grateful to Nando for the opportunity to appear in this workbook and to have been a part of the exploration of the articulation of the included techniques. I believe his ability to speak clearly regarding the often complex and seemingly obfuscated language of T'ai Chi into terms and experiences that I am able to relate to have made my learning curve (and hopefully yours) as easy as is possible. I am, however, most thankful for the gift and power of T'ai Chi and the internal changes that have occurred in me through this practice.

Now back to Nando...

How to use the workbook:

This book is designed for the beginning and intermediate push hands (t'ui shou) player. Frequently, push hands is not taught until after the student has learned the empty handed T'ai Chi Chuan form or at least in conjunction with learning the form. Thus I generally assume that you, the reader, know an empty handed T'ai Chi form. Do not be too concerned if you are coming to this material as a neophyte or from another martial arts tradition, however. There will be some small points you might not catch, but the drills and techniques described here will still make sense and be of value.

There is a gap in the written material publicly available in English on this topic. I am attempting to fill that by presenting a broad variety of progressive drills that systematically build skills. The drills come primarily from the Yang style with some from the Chen and Wu styles.

I have tried to demystify the development of basic push hands skills. By practicing these drills, you will improve your coordination and your ability to respond to the movements of a partner. This is the mundane level. If you practice them with persistent attention on the underlying T'ai Chi skills, energies, or "jings", you will gain far more.

There are limits, however, to what you can learn from this book. Use this book to understand the movements and practice until you can execute them with sensitivity and coordination. Use the stress of partner work to test and improve your body structure. At that point, if you are interested in further study, please seek contact with a skilled teacher. Seek a person who can demonstrate the skills and also has students who can demonstrate the skills! The more subtle T'ai Chi skills require careful personalized instruction to truly understand and develop them.

The first section of this book is an introduction and overview and the next sections are descriptions and photos of specific drills and games. It is, of course, best to learn push hands under the supervision of a qualified teacher. This workbook is for those who do not have that opportunity, those who want to speed their learning, or for instructors who want some tips and ideas for how to teach this material. If you are currently studying with an instructor, it is best to get his/her blessing on using this workbook.

In any case, even if you are currently taking a push hands class, recognize that there is rarely enough time to practice adequately in formal classes, so find interested fellow students and set aside times to play outside class.

The explorations, drills and games are presented in a progressive format. You will benefit the most if you practice them in order. Take the time to study the instructions and photos with care – it requires attention to learn a movement from a written description. Expect this and be patient with the process. Once you have learned a drill or game, keep it in mind as means for improving the specific skills in question and return to it from time to time.

Do several of them in each practice session in order to keep your study rich. Drills generally require more self-discipline, so I find it useful to do them first and then refresh myself with the greater freedom of games.

Train with diligence and persistence and improvement is guaranteed. The skills push hands develops take practice to become automatic. People generally agree that the time it takes to really get good at this is measured in years. Pay attention to making your practice time fun and rewarding so that you will want to do it! The material covered in this volume is for fixed step push hands. Most people can work through these fixed step drills and develop a moderate level of skill in 50 to 75 hours of practice. As you advance, these drills will remain useful, although (to reiterate) at some point developing higher levels of skill will almost certainly require individual instruction.

The photos:

Please understand that some of the photos do not reflect correct angles and distancing as sometimes adjustments did need to be made to properly display the arms, legs and hands. We shot these in shorts, t-shirts and without shoes to more clearly display the body. Some people and schools prefer greater formality or certain dress and foot wear codes.

The layout:

Some pages are intentionally partially blank to allow the text and photos of the subsequent section to flow well together.

Chapter 1

Introduction to Push Hands:

Push Hands (t'ui shou) is the name most often used to describe a variety of two person exercises used in T'ai Chi Chuan to train the fundamental skills which eventually lead to free sparring and effective physical self-defense. As there are many styles of T'ai Chi, so there are many different styles of push hands.

You may have heard the joke:
- How many T'ai Chi players does it take to change a light bulb?
-Just one, but the others stand around and say "That's good, but in my school we do it a little differently."
If you have studied push hands before, chances are you have done it differently.

Many people who practice T'ai Chi know little of push hands. This is a pity, because whereas practicing form can build balance, coordination, improve health and be a moving meditation, much of normal life is about interaction with others. Push hands is the opportunity to apply the attention and sensitivity learned in form practice to human interactions. Solo practice can help you be very sensitive, perceptive and open to your own experience, but it will not necessarily teach you how to use those skills interpersonally.

Some people see push hands as the more martial side of T'ai Chi and this turns them off. Personally, I find solo form practice of limited value when done without an understanding of the martial application. Push hands is a way to deepen that understanding and to test whether your structure and balance can stand up to the increased stress of interacting with another. Many people find that when stressed in a physical (or verbal) interaction, their carefully cultivated habits of staying centered get lost. Push hands will help with this.

Unfortunately, those who can benefit the most from push hands – those who are socially shy or awkward, or who are uncomfortable with physical interaction and touch – are usually the least likely to play in this way.

In addition to the physical skills of push hands, I've personally found the social and interpersonal skills developed from doing these drills and games to be invaluable. As a teacher, I have used push hands to good effect in psychologically oriented workshops to study the interactions between couples and to help strangers get to know each other. As we as a society develop a greater understanding of the importance of emotional and social intelligence (see Daniel Goldman's books), I hope that push hands will be increasingly valued for what it can contribute to these as well.

Explorations, Drills and Games:

I present three types of activities in this book – explorations, drills and games. Explorations are activities to do once or twice to experience something. Drills are activities to do again and again to hone skill and build confidence in yourself and your art. Games are playful combinations of many skills that foster spontaneity and discovery.

T'ai Chi, like most sports, has many drills. Any complex activity can benefit from drills that work on specific component skills. However, please distinguish between practicing the component skills and actually doing the activity. For instance, in learning a musical instrument, you might practice scales – these train an important skill. Playing scales, however, is not your goal, playing music is. Similarly, the activities in this workbook will improve both your push hands skills and your T'ai Chi in general. And at the next level, my hope is that through improving these skills, you will have a happier and more rewarding life.

Attentive practice of the drills will improve your overall game. Through repetition, however, drills become boring. Part of sensible practice is to spend some time on drills and some time on free play. As you advance, so do the appropriate drills and the complexity of the games.

Usually in the game of push-hands each person is trying to cause the other to lose balance. In the drills, on the other hand, knocking your partner off balance is often an error. The game, with its playful competitiveness, is enticing, but if you want to really understand push hands and be good at it, do the drills as drills! Train to perfect your sensitivity and movement as well as to play the game better.

In any case, push hands practice is an important aspect of training because it is in the confrontation with another that our skills are really tested. Just how good is your balance? Just how sensitive and relaxed are you? How much frustration can you tolerate before you become angry and tense? How much fun can you have competing while not hurting yourself or your partner?

Before we get into the actual drills, we'll briefly consider a few points.

Push Hands and Self-Defense:

Ultimately push hands is designed to train perceptual and movement skills for fighting. Yet, through the exercise of care and the blessing of good fortune, we hope never to be in this situation. Physically, we are training for something that we hope will never happen. Mentally and emotionally, we are training to raise our awareness and our social skills to reduce the likelihood that we will ever need our physical skills. (For more discussion of self-defense, please see the article in the appendix.)

The highest level of self-defense is preventing violence and preserving life. Doing so is based on being sufficiently aware and centered so that you listen to your intuition don't go down that street so that you are never attacked in the first place. This is both an external and internal sensitivity issue. First you must perceive the danger, then you must value and honor your felt sense of apprehension. In this way we can understand "when my partner moves, I move first".

Basic physical combat skills are easier to learn than good push hands, but they do not necessarily train the interpersonal sensitivity that is fundamental to push hands. Interpersonal sensitivity and flexibility is profoundly useful in daily life while physical combat skills are not.

Although I enjoy the self-defense aspects of push hands, the highest value I have received has been in the areas of improved structure, confrontation of my own pride and ego, developing greater emotional and social intelligence, and interpersonal sensitivity.

Push Hands Competition:

In the past few decades, there have been push hands competitions in the United States at T'ai Chi tournaments. There is a natural desire for people to want an external gauge of how their skills are progressing. However, if your attention is on winning a competition, this may or may not also develop the deeper skills you are seeking.

Tournament push hands has become more standardized, but rules still vary. The winners may be the people who have trained within those rules, not the most skilled. In past competitions, some winners have been wrestlers who have little of the sensitivity we train in T'ai Chi. Current rules are formulated to reduce that likelihood. If you are interested in the rules you can find them on the internet.

As you will see as you play more advanced games, trying to win can actually undermine the deeper skills you are seeking to cultivate. (For more discussion on competition and push hands, see Herman Kauz's book.)

Humility and Good Humor:

To be willing to confront your own vulnerability and truly "invest in loss" (a favorite saying of Cheng Man-Ch'ing's), it is very helpful to cultivate humility and good humor in push hands. By remaining humble, you will be less likely to be trapped into self-protective (defensive) tension. Humility will also allow you to stay present and not get seduced into arrogance. To be able to learn, you must first admit to yourself that you do not know everything and are not perfectly skilled. I'm sure you too have had interactions with people who are so defensive (about their movement, beliefs or emotions) that they are not willing to allow themselves the vulnerability of openly receiving a learning experience.

Good humor will allow you to not get bent out of shape (physically and emotionally) when you get knocked over. After all, it is only a game. So practice laughing and complimenting your partner when she knocks you over. This will help you relax, which in turn will help you stay flexible and responsive. Humor also antidotes the physical arousal and stress of having your balance challenged. With humor, you will be more able to enjoy push hands as a cooperative game instead of as a struggle for dominance and status. As your skill improves, you will be able to maintain your good humor in increasingly stressful situations. This attitude can serve you well if you are ever actually attacked, allowing you more clarity of mind.

Push Hands as a Metaphor for Relationship:

In my capacity as a marriage and mental health counselor, I have always been intrigued by what push hands has to teach us about relationship. As you push with different people, you become more able to perceive their character through their movement. How does this person deal with being pushed – do they move against or away, do they twist or become solid? How do you feel being pushed by them? What is required to get in synch with them in a drill?

There is a tremendous amount of information available for you to receive in these interactions. Do you receive it? Much of it will be intuitive – experienced as a non-articulated sense or image of the other person. I encourage you to unpack this intuition into words so that you can understand it - do not ignore this information just because it is not yet in a verbal format!

In addition to what you learn about others, there is also a tremendous opportunity to confront your own character defects, buttons and hang-ups. Generally these get in the way of accurately perceiving others. The requirement to be sensitive to others in push hands forces us to reduce the internal noise generated by our own personality. Allowing internal dialogue and moodiness is the surest way to take yourself out of the moment and thus find yourself knocked over.

The Spiritual Side of Push Hands:

As you develop greater sensitivity to others and improve your ability to be present under interpersonal stress, you will perceive more deeply into the heart and intent of yourself and others.

If your interest is in chi kung or healing, chi will become more perceptible through this practice.

If your interest is in being more present, in the now, and connected to the Tao, the physical challenge of push hands will give you rapid physical feedback about when you drift away. Nothing focuses the mind like the physical danger of falling over or being hit!

Ideally, you will also develop compassion through this practice, as you learn to push others over with loving kindness and to lift yourself off the ground with the same attitude.

Personally, I find it helpful to structure my whole life around a consistent set of principles. If something does not make sense to me in one area of my life, then it brings this same thing into question in another area. The core principle is:

There is a way (Tao) that things work. If I align myself with that with awareness and coordination, freedom is available in each moment.

Solo form T'ai Chi is the place where I study the (mostly) physical awareness and coordination issues of having this body. Partner T'ai Chi is the place where I study relationship issues in the same way.

Epiphanies and insights I obtain through my practice must then be intentionally applied to and crosschecked with the mental, emotional, and spiritual realms.

The Roles of Attacker and Defender:

Push hands games work because one person is attacking and the other is defending. Paradoxically, if both partners were really embodying T'ai Chi principles in their lives, there would be no attacker. But in order to play and train, we need someone to attack. If you have ever seen an Aikido demonstration, you know what I mean. The attacker runs at the master, who uses the determination and momentum of the attacker to defeat him. This is exactly what happens in partner T'ai Chi demonstrations, where the master sends his attacker flying. This also happen in many T'ai Chi drills. If neither person actually attacks, the drills often do not work.

There is a place for being very cautious in your attack, and this caution becomes ingrained over years of practice. But often your willingness to push your partner is a gift for them. In teaching, I will frequently "give" my partner something to defend against. On the other hand, when you push slowly and precisely through your partner's center, he will have little defense that does not rely on force against force or some little trick. Once you reach a certain level, you can almost always push your partner over if you push slowly and he follows the rules.

Pushing your partner over is great for training his willingness to "invest in loss", one of CMC's training adages. But don't be too annoying! This is particularly true when working with those less experienced than you. Give your partner a "stupid" push that is stiff, off center or overextended so he has something to work with. Were you really intent on hurting him, this is probably what your push would be like. So give him an honest attack, and ask for one back.

When you push with someone less skilled than you, they will often push in a forceful way that you can neutralize early. In order to make the partnership more challenging for you, allow your partner to push you further back to where you have less room to neutralize.

Physical Closeness:

Most of the fixed step drills presented here are done in a same sided forward stance where the forward feet are parallel. In this way, the area where each person has the most power (a forward biased oval passing on the outside of each foot) overlap.

Push hands is generally done at this distance, but recognize that you get more mechanical advantage if you can put your center where your partner's used to be. This shows up more in moving step drills (see Chapter 7), but even at this distance, any hesitation you have to touch and become physically and perceptually involved with your partner will undermine your ability to influence his center.

You are more at risk and also stronger if you really invade your partner's space. If you are squeamish or too polite about this, it will undermine your effectiveness in these drills and games and also hamper you in a real self defense situation. If you hesitate to connect with your partner's armpit, how much more will you hesitate to connect with an unkempt drunken attacker?

Get over this in these drills and shower and wash your hands afterwards!

Gender:

In general, it is helpful to have men pair with women and vice versa for effective push hands partnerships. This helps maintain balance between yin and yang in the relationship. This is, of course, based on generalizations that may not apply to your specific situation.

Male/male partnerships are often too yang, and the partners may get trapped in competition and in using force against force. They may not be willing to be emotionally or physically vulnerable with one another and this may limit the learning that takes place.

Female/female partnerships can be too yin, where the players do not challenge each other strongly and hesitate to push each other strongly.

Male/female partners tend to balance the energy in each other in a way that is mutually beneficial.

(In the text that follows, I will use the gender pronouns he and she interchangeably when not referring to photos.)

Creating an Effective Push Hands Partnership:

There will be some push hands relationships that work better for you than others. What is that about and how can you find and create a really good partnership?

The quality of relationship you have with your push hands partners will determine how willing you are to be physically and emotionally vulnerable with them. To really learn this material, you must be vulnerable, so it pays to create good working relationships.

Emotional issues are guaranteed to arise as you practice push hands. After all, your partner is trying to push you over! It is easy to get annoyed and uptight if you are consistently "losing" or you may just not be comfortable having this person or energy in your "space". Additionally, it is not unusual to be confronted with your own fear, anger or self-judgment when practicing push hands.

Because of this, it is important to have a partner with whom you feel comfortable. Consider how aggressive, competitive and sensitive your partner is. If you can find a partner with whom you feel emotionally, as well as physically, safe, you will feel comfortable sharing and exploring more personal aspects of your training and it will be a far richer experience for you.

Much of the T'ai Chi training curriculum is based on slowly increasing the level of stress within which you can relax. Once you can relax in the simpler push-hand drills, learn more complex ones. Humans learn best when they feel safe enough, so train in a manner that keeps your anxiety low.

Your learning edge will be close to the point where you lose physical or emotional balance, so it is helpful to "invest in loss" and train at that place. For example, find a partner who truly challenges you and then openly study how, precisely, you feel challenged. This may entail asking your partner to push you over in the same sort of way twenty times. Truly investing in loss may be harder on your sense of pride than your body!

When choosing a partner, pay attention to these issues:

- Power, weight and skill – Who is likely to be pushing who over? An intermediate 110 pound person can be overpowered by a novice 200 pound person. Have realistic expectations about what you can gain and offer in the interaction.

- Pride and competitiveness – The learning partnership that will work best has a manageable level of these elements. It is easy to find a partner who is so emotionally stuck in pride or competitiveness that he is unable to do cooperative drills. Might you be one of these people? Assess yourself and your partner honestly here. I have been knocked over repeatedly by people in ways that were helpful and by others in ways that were humiliating. Why play with people who are so stuck they need to humiliate?

- Communication skills – It is so helpful to be able to put words on our experience! This is true whether it is an internal physical or emotional process or about an interaction. Have realistic expectations of yourself and your partner, but work on this aspect as well as the movements.

Internal aspects of these skills: I find it useful to view myself as composed of psychologically different parts. For instance, I may have a part of myself making comments on my performance. Some people are very familiar with their "inner critic". We know that the best external learning atmosphere is marked by relaxation, respect and awareness. The same is true for the internal environment. Internal criticism for either party can sour a push hands session. So practice listening, and being respectful, non-defensive, and compassionate inside as well as with your partner! I guarantee this will lead to faster and deeper learning.

Chapter 2

Movement Fundamentals/Principles:

Read through this and familiarize yourself with these terms and basics before you try the push hands movements. If you are an experienced T'ai Chi player, this material will probably be review for you. I encourage you to skim through it nonetheless since I probably use a slightly different terminology than what you are accustomed to.

With any sport or physical activity, a solid understanding of the basics is the foundation upon which further progress is built. Even for profoundly skilled, world class athletes, often the way to make further progress is to return to the basics once again. T'ai Chi push hands is no different. Beginners should study and practice these basics and return to them again and again as their practice deepens.

In T'ai Chi, the basics are the Principles, which are discussed in the Classics, the core canon of T'ai Chi writings. There are a number of different translations of these (see Yang, Jwing Ming, Fu Zhongwen, Ben Lo) and different teachers and translators often add their commentaries. I find it useful to distinguish between fundamental principles, postural and energy requirements, and directives that are specific to the solo form or to partner work. I offer this here for your consideration. At the same time, the Classics have been written, translated and commented on by people far more skilled than I, so please also read the original sources to avoid my errors.

The fundamental principles and postural, movement and energy requirements apply to all T'ai Chi forms including slow and fast sets, weapons forms and partner work. Movements that do not follow these are not T'ai Chi.

Principles:
- The body is relaxed (song), using the least amount of force necessary for any given action.
- The body moves naturally.
- The mind is calm and alert; the intent directs chi and movement.

Postural, Movement and Energy Requirements (from the ground up):
- Connect through the Bubbling Well point (Kidney 1, just towards the heel from the ball of the foot) into the earth.
- Bend and soften the ankles and knees and sit at the hip joints – these are shock absorbers.
- *Song* (relax and sink) the waist.
- Sink the chi (vitality and attention) to the tan tien (two finger thicknesses down from the navel in the middle of the body), move from the tan tien (your center of gravity).
- The spine is upright, the tailbone hangs, the perineum is relaxed.
- Soften and sink the chest, allowing the back to rise and round.
- *Song* (relax and sink) the shoulders and arms.
- Tongue touches the roof of the mouth.
- Float the head as if suspended from the bahui point (crown).

- Eyes in soft focus, leading the movement.
- Breathe naturally and deeply into the abdomen.
- Keep the body connected – if one part moves, everything moves, if one part stops, the whole body stops.
- Distinguish yin from yang, substantial/solid/weighted and insubstantial/unweighted.

Points for solo form practice:
- Move slowly and evenly, with no stops and starts.
- Seek stillness (of mind) in movement.

Additional points for partner practice:
- Stick to your partner, do not avoid or separate from her.
- Wait for her to initiate and follow her movement.
- Do not oppose or resist her movement, but by joining and following gain a superior position (arrive first).

I'll just say a few things about the basics of relaxation, sensitivity, breathing, and then come back to movement mechanics, correct posture and going with your partner's movement.

Relaxation:

In T'ai Chi, the movements are performed with the maximum amount of relaxation possible while still accomplishing the intent of the movement. The Chinese term is "song", which has connotations of relaxation, looseness, and heaviness. Some muscle tone is required even to simply stand upright and breathe, so we do not want to eliminate all muscular activity. Instead we want to eliminate any excess tension.

Tight muscles immobilize joints. Loose enough muscles allow joints to move. Relaxation is balanced by the requirement to move the whole body as one unit. The latter is done by maintaining physical connection between body parts. This requires some muscle tone.

Relaxing is a skill. Functional relaxation is very different from simply collapsing. Muscular relaxation actually requires energy (in the form of the biochemical energy molecule ATP). This is why corpses stiffen in rigor – the muscles have used up the ATP. I include in the appendix an article on learning to relax.

Sensitivity:

The correct performance of T'ai Chi requires being open and attentive to your sensations. Some sensations may originate from body position or breathing, but some of the sensations arise from the flow of your Chi and changes of your attention. In partner work, many blatant and subtle sensations arise from the interaction. Since in T'ai Chi we are trying to accomplish our goals with the minimum amount of force and tension, naturally we must be perceptive and intelligent both in receiving and applying energy.

Recognize that your attention can be clear or cluttered. A busy mind, filled with worries about the past and the future, is not going to be able to pay as good attention to the present moment as a still mind. Use meditative techniques to slow yourself down mentally and reduce the internal noise you are generating. In this way you will be more able to perceive your partner (and the present moment in general).

Physical tension also reduces sensitivity. The classics say that one should stand balanced like a scale such that not even a fly can alight without creating movement. This level of sensitivity requires extreme relaxation. According to Weber's Law, the minimum perceptible change in a stimulus is proportional to the intensity of the stimulus; if the stimulus is large, we need a proportionally larger change before it becomes perceptible (see Chuckrow). Thus guitars are best tuned quietly and as our contact with our partner has more pressure we are less able to perceive their subtle changes. Your contact with your partner, even when pushing, should remain light and perceptive.

Breathing:

The breath is very important in T'ai Chi. In the form it is used to set and slow the tempo of movement. It is the most obvious mind/body connection and an important access point for your study of the Tao (the way of life). Physiologically, it is both the easiest way to calm the body and often the first place that tension shows up. In push hands, when you are emotionally upset or in a precarious position, often you will find yourself holding or limiting your breath. Expect this and use purposeful deep, full, slow breathing to give yourself physical and emotional space.

Although some people practice differently, I find it most useful to inhale as I yield, and exhale as I express energy. No matter what the phase of your breath, by keeping your breath relaxed and even, you will help calm your mind and keep your movement more fluid and connected.

You are more vulnerable to attack at the transitions points between your inhale and exhale. By keeping your breathing smooth and silent, you will protect yourself and be more likely to hear your partner's breath.

I recommend that my students practice reverse breathing when doing their form and also while doing push hands. For those of you not familiar with this term, we distinguish between normal, "post birth" or "Buddhist" breathing and reverse, "prebirth' or "Taoist" breathing.

In normal breathing, the inhale stacks from the belly up the front of the body, the diaphragm drops, pushes out the belly, and then the breath fills the solar plexus area and finally the chest. During the exhale, the lungs empty from the top first, and the abdomen draws in at the end. Natural, full, relaxed breathing follows this pattern. This is called diaphragmatic breathing in the West. It is called Buddhist because this is the breath used in most Buddhist sitting meditation.

Try this exploration: Stand facing a wall with one foot forward and both hands on it so that you can push against it easily. While relaxed and comfortable, without pushing, take a few deep breaths paying attention to the movement of your abdomen and chest. Next, maintain a push against the wall with about ten pounds of pressure and take a few more deep breaths. Notice the difference in the movement of your chest and abdomen.

In order to support the horizontal pressure at the shoulder girdle from pushing, you had to increase the tone in your abdomen. This occurs whenever we brace to do physical work. When the abdomen is toned, the compression of the internal organs that occurs with the dropping of the diaphragm on the inhale causes expansion to the sides and back at the waist. As you continue to inhale, the abdomen goes in as the breath fills the back of the chest. If you are trying to maximize power, you will also probably bear down a bit on the exhale, pushing the internal organs into the pelvic bowl and expanding the entire waist area.

This is called "reverse breathing" because the abdomen moves in the reverse sequence as during relaxed, "normal" breathing. It's called "prebirth" because it's the breath pattern that happens when you are in a fetal position. And it is called "Taoist" because this breath is often used in qigong practices as well as in T'ai Chi.

When you do this breathing, and particularly if you bear down on the exhale, blood from the abdomen is pushed into the extremities, including the head. This may cause a perceptible change in blood pressure in the head. Since blood pools in the abdomen during the "fight or flight" activation of the autonomic nervous system, this type of breathing counteracts this arousal, helping to relax the body and oxygenate the brain.

I want to stress that this breath occurs naturally when you do physical work. It is not some new esoteric practice you have to learn. When you practice your form, you will naturally find yourself breathing this way if your legs are properly bracing and you are moving the whole body as one unit.

This is an important point, so let me repeat myself. Rather than teaching my students to force their breath into this pattern, I ask them to do enough work (bracing their legs and moving as one unit) so that the natural tone in the abdomen creates this breath pattern. As you develop better structural and coordination habits, less and less muscle tone is required to maintain them.

It is essential to maintain leg structure and whole body movement in push hands, so you should naturally find yourself doing reverse breathing.

For more on Taoist breathing practices see Mantak Chia's work and for an introduction to Heng – Haah breathing see Master Jou's The Tao of Tai-Chi Chuan.

Now let's return to our exploration of posture, stances and fundamental movement dynamics.

Correct posture:

For maximum relaxation, sensitivity and power, there are postural requirements for each part of the body. However the unifying theme is to put the body in the shape where it can be filled with vitality. Imagine the body as a water hose, and then make sure there are no kinks, so that as the water begins to flow, it is not blocked. Over time, you will become familiar with how your joints feel when your chi is flowing freely and how they feel when it is blocked. This requires the joints to be loose and open; the posture erect; the breathing full; and the heart, mind and facial expression open. In addition, feel and imagine yourself rooted to the earth. This is accomplished by keeping the joints of the legs open and springy, by opening the pelvic floor, by firming the legs as if braced against the rocking of a ship and by visualizing your energetic connection with the center of the earth.

The classics say to keep the body upright and the head as if suspended from the heavens. In push hands, you make yourself vulnerable when you lean to the sides or back. However a slight incline forward can at times actually help you maintain a stable posture under pressure from the front. I will periodically remind you about "body upright". I do not mean to imply that the body should be plumb erect, but rather that the center line should be sufficiently plumb so that you can twist without knocking yourself off balance.

Truly correct posture only begins with the external requirements of precise placement. Once you have a good sense of what you are trying to do, then modify the externally dictated correct posture to truly fit your own body. Be gentle with yourself as you perfect your T'ai Chi movements. They are designed to be comfortable for all people, but you may need to modify them slightly to make them really work for you. This is a reason why personal instruction can be especially important.

Let's look now at some common leg and arm stances and positions.

Stances:
It is best to think of stances as common transitory positions the body moves through, as opposed to static postures.

In all the stances, seek to create a very stable platform from the navel and pelvis down upon which the upper body can rest. Once the platform is created, use your breath to create a sense of spaciousness and lift in the upper body. The breath is full and deep into the lower abdomen, the shoulders rest on the rib cage, and the neck is free to allow the head to float. The chin is slightly dropped, the tongue touches the roof of the mouth lightly (to close an energy circuit between the Conception and Governing Meridians and to help relax the lower jaw) and the head floats as if suspended from the crown. Cultivate a sense of sinking and spaciousness in the pelvic floor.

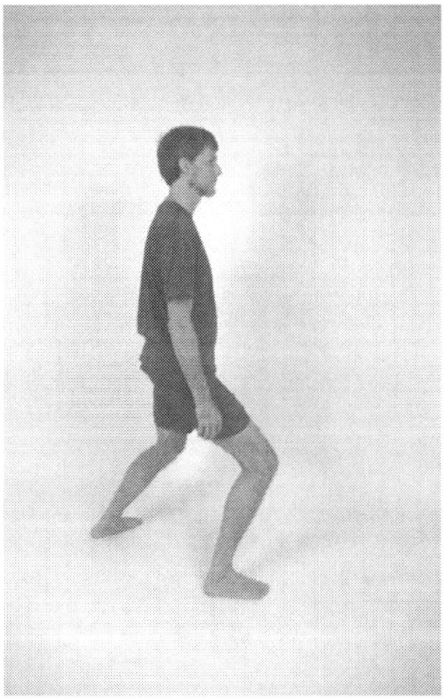

Photo 1

16

Stances can be quite low, with a lot of bend in the knee and sitting in the hip joint (photo 1) or quite high (photo 2). It is important that each student seek a level at which he or she is comfortable. Lower stances are better exercise. Higher stances are more nimble.

Serious martial artists use lower stances for strength and flexibility training while generally sparring in higher stances. A good way to test your height is to establish a stance, shift the weight totally into one leg, staying at the same level, and lift the other foot an inch off the ground. If you can do it with good balance and control, this height is ok for you. Try it again a little lower until you run into the limit where you can no longer lift the other leg easily.

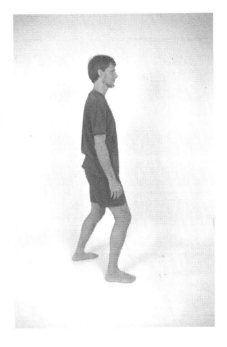

If you use a lower stance, the length will be greater. The width generally remains the same, but the length will change with how deeply you sit in your hips and bend your knees.

The use of your hips and legs is a critically important aspect of posture. Only when you have a solid structure from the navel down though the pelvis to your feet will you really feel comfortable and allow your energy to flow. This structural concern is common in many martial arts and Qigong as well. The general requirements of feet, leg and pelvis shape apply to all the stances.

Photo 2

In our stance work, we are seeking to create a structure that can withstand a load. If your bones and joints are not held in the correct position by your muscles, they will not be able to take the load when it is applied and your body will use its innate wisdom to protect itself. This may show up as falling, crumpling, distorting, or simply as weakness. Honor the wisdom of your body – if you experience any of these defects correct them by improving your structure and alignment.

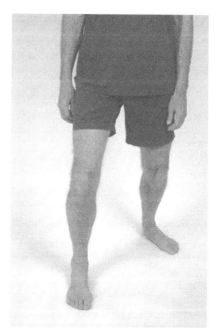

Sometimes the best way to get the correct alignment and structure is to do a little isometrics. I call this "bracing". It is what you do naturally in your legs when you stand on a ship or a moving train. Bracing uses a small isometric tone to put the bones in position to take a sudden load.

In the leg, the weakest point is usually the knee. As a consequence, the structural requirements of the knee dictate the way we use our legs (for some people the weakest joint may be the ankle). The knee is a hinge joint, and as with metal hinges, if the hinge is twisted as it opens and closes it will eventually break. Pay precise attention to keeping the bones of the upper and lower legs in line so that the knee is not twisted. Compare these photos where the weight is forward: #3 is correct. In #4 the forward knee is twisted out, peeling the big toe of the forward foot off the ground. To avoid this, make sure that the navel points the same direction as the weighted thigh, knee and foot.

Photo 3

Photo 4

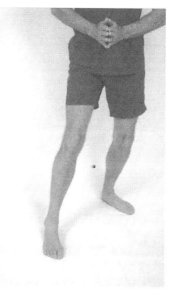

In #5, the weight is back and the knee is supported by the navel and thigh going in the same direction as the weighted foot. In #6 the rear knee is now twisted with the navel and thigh. To prevent this, keep the navel pointed in the same direction as the weighted thigh, knee and foot.

It is, unfortunately, very common to see T'ai Chi players violating this rule during form practice. The error is even more common in partner work. Practice in a way that prevents knee strain and injuries. Through careful attention to these points, my students have had no knee troubles. As you become more advanced and your

Photo 5

Photo 6

body becomes stronger and more integrated you will not need to be as careful about this as in the beginning.

Protecting your knee joints requires that you spread or round the crotch so that rather than feeling like the legs meet at the pelvis in an upside down V, you feel them meeting as an upside down U. If you do this and keep the feet at the width of the hip joints, the leg bones will be in alignment and the knees and ankles should feel comfortable.

Once in this shape, brace the legs slightly as if you are on the deck of a ship that is moving with the waves. By bracing slightly in the legs, you will feel more solid and are more able to respond to whatever the future may hold. Bracing corrects the problem illustrated in photo #7 where the weight is forward and the rear knee is collapsed. In this collapsed stance, the rear little toe will start to roll off the ground and you will feel weak.

To know the stance you are seeking, I strongly encourage you to practice the correct feeling and also to do it wrong on purpose a couple times so that you have a clear experience of what you want to avoid.

Photo 7

Forward stance:
The most common stance used in Yang style push hands is a "bow and arrow" or forward stance. Here the forward foot faces your partner and the rear foot is turned out 30' – 45'. The rear foot is positioned so that there is hip width between the heels parallel to the inside line of the forward foot (see fig.1). The length of the stance is determined by how far forward you can reach the free heel while standing balanced in the rear leg. Maintain your spine upright,

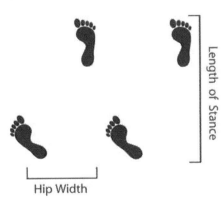

reach the free heel out and then roll onto it as you shift forward. Make sure that the heel, big toe and little toe of each foot are on the floor and that 70% of the weight is in the balls of the feet. As you become more comfortable with push hands, experiment with the stance to see if some small modification can make it even more comfortable for you.

When the weight is forward, the knee should not go past (forward of) the toes. And as mentioned above, care of the knees requires that the bones of the thigh be on the same vertical plane as the bones of the lower leg. This usually requires the navel to face the same direction as the weighted

Hip Width

Length of Stance

Fig. 1

foot. Because you will be shifting weight back and forth during most of these movements, attention to this is very important. When your weight is forward the navel should face forward.

As you shift your weight back, your navel should turn to the side to face the same direction as the rear foot and thigh. As you shift back and forth, the pelvis will naturally turn to allow the weighted thigh to go in the same direction as the weighted foot. This is called following the hip track.

Exploration:

As you become more flexible in your hip joints, you will be able to move the navel away from the line of the legs without twisting the knee. This exploration is to help you to find your current personal range of motion experimentally.

Photo 8   Stand with the heels hip width   Photo 9
                           apart with one leg forward in a
standard forward stance, weight mostly forward. With the hands resting on the
hips or shoulders (to get them out of the way), twist the body slowly through the torso. Lead your twist with your eyes and see how far you can go in each direction without allowing the twist to displace your knee. For some people it can be helpful to have a partner physically hold the knee in place during the twist. Feel how you adjust in the hips and through the legs to keep your knee in place. Photo # 8 shows this done with properly braced legs, #9 shows the twist going down the legs creating discomfort and instability.

Do this exercise again with the weight mostly back and then with the weight in the middle. Then switch feet and do it on the other side. Use these to educate yourself on the feeling of keeping your knee stable as you twist.

When you do this motion, the inguinal area (the front of the hips at the groin where the thigh meets the pelvis) opens and closes. This area is called the "kua" and its motion is a primary source of the power of opening and closing.

Twisting, or rotation around the midline, must be done in the kua, waist and torso, not in a way that stresses the knees and ankles. Once you have a solid feel of being braced and keeping the knee stable while twisting through the torso from the exercise above, you should be able to move back and forth while twisting without stressing your knees or undermining your own balance.

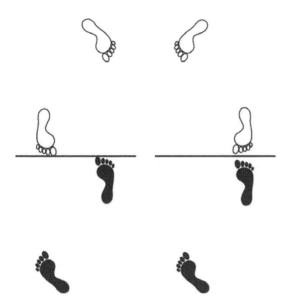

Figure 2: Enclosed and open stances

Most of the push hands drills and games in this book are done with both people in forward stances, the line of the front foot facing each other. Same sided forward stances (also called enclosed stances) have both partners with their right (or left) foot forward. The left of fig. 2 shows this. Mirror sided forward stances (also called open or direct stances) are less common and have one person with his right foot forward and the other with her left forward. The right of fig. 2 shows this. The feet of the people in this figure show them standing relatively far apart. This is a good starting distance for many drills. As we will discuss a little later, moving your forward foot a few inches forward can make quite a difference.

Some people choose to offset their stance a little to their partner. That is, they will turn their front foot and the whole stance a little to their inside. This offers some protection for the groin and can be useful as you become more experienced. On the other hand, it closes off the line of your push a bit. I recommend starting with your forward foot parallel with your partner's as shown in the figure.

The exercises in the next chapter will build your understanding of stance work even more, but for now let's discuss arms.

Arm Structures:
Through proper foot placement and bracing the legs, you have made the pelvis into a stable platform. The bends at the ankles, knees and hips give the platform springy support. The spine is rooted in this platform and is free to twist. The shoulder girdle rests on the rib cage and anchors the arms to the spine. The hands and arms are used both as sense organs and tools for affecting your partner. Power arises from the legs pressing against the earth, this power is channeled through the pelvis, directed by the waist and torso, and expressed through the arms and hands.

In order to serve as sense organs, the arms and hands must be soft and the joints easily moved. In order to serve as tools they must be firm and the bones must be positioned to be able to take a load. These are, to a certain degree, contradictory to one another (a movement dialectic). It is up to you to balance and manifest both the yin and yang of this.

Shoulder Down to Elbow Up to Wrist: This general rule for arm structure reminds you to keep the elbows down and weighted (song) in order to ensure that the shoulder blades remain connected through the latissimus dorsi muscles (lats) to the rib cage and the body as a whole. Unless the arm is raised so high that the elbow must be higher than the shoulder, the line of the arm goes down from shoulder to elbow. And unless the hand is so low that the wrist must be lower than the elbow, the line then goes up to the wrist. Generally the angle at the elbow is greater than 90' to give the arm the strength of the extensor muscles.

Specific Arm Structures:

Photo 10

Ward Off (Peng): (see photo 10) This is a posture using one or both arms where the arm is in an arc in front of the body with the palm facing the center line at about the level of the base of the sternum. By hollowing the chest slightly (extending the rhomboids), force received on the forearm can be channeled through the shoulder blades to the spine. The arm(s) follow the "shoulder down to elbow up to wrist" rule. This posture is used as an extra layer of protection between you and the incoming energy. It can also be used as a posture to attack with the forearm.

Peng is a central energy in T'ai Chi and should be present in all of the movements. We can think of it as the energy inside an inflated balloon or the energy we adopt when pushing through a crowd. Having braced the legs, we then extend the arms and fill the torso with peng energy to create an even more stable and resilient structure. You can also understand peng as the solidity of the ground propagated through the body thanks to correct alignment (see Sigman).

Roll Back (Lu): This is both a posture in the solo form and a process. When your partner pushes and you catch her push on a ward off and then shift back and turn on your midline, this is called roll back. You behave like a beach ball being pushed under water, sinking and spinning, and this can help you achieve a superior position.

Photo 11

Two Handed Push (An): (photo 11) Position yourself as if pushing a van out of a ditch. The arms follow the "shoulder down to elbow up to wrist" rule and the palms face away from the body as wide as the shoulders with the finger tips no higher than the shoulders. When the weight is back, allow the lower spine to round with the tailbone a little tucked under to create a solid structural connection between the legs and arms. The energy for the push comes from extending the rear leg to shift the weight forward. When you do that, the angles at shoulder and elbow should not change much.

One Handed Push: (photo 12) This posture is the same as the two handed push method done with only one hand. As a consequence, the pushing hand must move closer to the midline in order to maintain power. The first knuckle of the thumb tends to be on the midline.

Press (Jhee): This posture has the outer arm in a ward off shape while the inner hand presses on the palm, wrist, forearm or elbow to support and augment the structure. This allows the power of both sides of the body to triangulate on a single point. Another translation of the Chinese term "jhee" is to squeeze, as in squeezing into a doorway. Here the rear hand is supporting the forward arm to squeeze into the small space between you and your partner (more on this later).

Using these postures and structures, let's look at the natural sources of relaxed power in the body.

Sources of Power:

In T'ai Chi push–hands, we avoid using strength to control our opponent. Instead, we are trying to train our use of "intrinsic" energy.

Photo 12

In "using 4 ounces to deflect 1000 pounds" (a phrase used in the T'ai Chi Classics to epitomize efficiency), we use core body strength. We make contact with the incoming force early and deflect it by applying the deflecting 4 ounces continually until it is past us. Sometimes the deflection moves our body away from the line of attack and sometimes it alters the attack. This is called "intrinsic" strength because it makes use of the strength of the core muscles of the legs, spine and waist (psoas, erector spinae, semispinalis, quadratus lumborum and obliques), the muscles that connect the shoulder blade to the trunk (latissimus dorsi, rhomboids and seratus anterior) and the extensor muscles of the arms and legs.

To feel this, catch your partner's push on your left ward off with your right foot forward as Brian is doing with me in photo 13. Brian is connecting to the outside of my left arm with the inside of his right arm. When you take Brian's position with a partner, the structure of your ward off arm will come from your braced legs, the positioning of the pelvis, lower back and sacrum, the strength of your deep waist muscles, the connection of you left arm through the latissimus dorsi (lats) to the torso and, finally, the extension of your left arm. As you roll back, which entails shifting your weight back to your left, turning left and transferring the turn into your partner's body with your extended right arm, you are applying the four ounces of deflection force by shifting with the legs and twisting

Photo 13

23

around your core. This type of strength is also called perceptive or sensitive strength because it is responsive to the precise needs of the moment and the vulnerability of your partner.

In contrast, we use "clumsy strength" or "li" when we take our partner by the shoulders and shift them bodily to the side as I am attempting to do to Brian in photo 14.. The effort here is performed primarily by the "extrinsic" muscles of the arms, shoulders and chest (biceps, deltoids and pectorals).

Many authors warn physically strong people against the trap of relying on li or clumsy strength. This is part of the whole strategy of investing in loss in order to build perceptual skills. It is very challenging to stick to the principles and "lose" when you know you could just use your muscle and "win".

In order to use intrinsic strength, it is helpful to recognize that there are only a few ways that we gain access to this. They are, in order of descending power: shifting the weight, turning the body, going up or down, and opening or closing. These are often combined for greater power.

Photo 14

Shifting the weight: as we move forward or back, we use the extensor muscles of the legs to generate momentum, and this can be applied to your partner. The movement "push" is primarily accomplished by shifting forward with some moving up.

Turning the body: this is accomplished by using the deep muscles of the abdomen with the support of the legs. Often this is combined with shifting the weight as when we shift back and turn in "roll back" and/or with opening or closing at the kua (inguinal crease) as in "split" at the end of "roll back".

Going up or down; here we straighten or bend the knees and hips to raise or drop the body to generate momentum. We go up at the end of the "push", in "white crane spreads wings" and in "play lute". We go down in "split", in "press", in "needle at sea bottom" and "squatting down".

Opening or closing; here we open or close the hip and shoulder joints. This is a weaker source of power and is almost always combined with one of the three above. Open and close is demonstrated in "lift hands" and we close in the "press".

It can be useful to study your form so that you are able to clearly discern and focus on these sources of your power. It is hard to apply your power strongly and with precision if you do not know where it is coming from.

If your structure is disorganized, your power will be weak and diffuse. Generally the errors are in leg structure and use of the waist. Your body, in its wisdom, will try to protect you from injury. If your leg structure is weak or your pelvis and waist poorly positioned, your body will undermine your power (without consulting you) to prevent injury.

So far we have been talking about how you use your body when alone. We'll finish this section by considering how to interact with another person's body and momentum.

Going With the Flow of Your Partner's Movement:

Taoist philosophy is based on the understanding that there is a "way" inherent in life, and that the wise path is to align oneself with that way. We're advised to follow the universal flow instead of trying to create our own flow in a headstrong fashion. A simple directive; the challenge is in the execution. In push hands, first we follow our own postural requirements, then we stick/adhere in order to accurately listen to, join with and follow our partner's movement in order to gain a superior position.

I had an epiphany about this one day at the beach playing in the waves off Oahu on a boogie board. If I was stationary, waves would crash over me, but if I could bring myself up close to their speed, they would sweep me along. As I got better at it, I could find the precise angle relative to the force of the wave that would maximize my ride. Taoism advises that we do this in the rest of life (and in push hands) as well.

There are some patterns of energy in our lives that are so obvious that they are fairly easy to ride - like a wave. But often, the more important and profound the current is, the more subtle one's perception must be to catch it. The flows of breath or chi are examples of relatively subtle rhythms. Your partner's movement is more obvious. In order to connect with and follow these flows, the challenge is twofold: 1) perceive it 2) connect with it without creating too much turbulence.

In my work as a psychotherapist, my first task is to establish rapport with my client. Only then will I have the credibility required to influence his or her life. In order to influence an energy, it is most effective to first attend to getting in synch with it. In order to catch those waves with my boogie board, I first had to approach their speed. I had to abandon my own willfulness and take my cues from them. Only then could I start to play with their energy. In push hands, I must first listen to my partner. Once the Yin portion of my activity (listening, establishing rapport, joining) is successful, then I can become more assertive (Yang).

Unless we first get in alignment with another energy, our contact will have a quality of collision to it, which from a push hands perspective is precisely what we are seeking to minimize. Imagine what might happen on the highway if you neglected to accelerate as you entered the freeway! In order to blend with already manifest flows of energy, we try to match them before we connect with them. I have to approach the speed of the wave to be able to ride it. I must already be moving with my partner before I try to influence his body.

Here is a way to explore this dynamic on your own through "full body breathing" chi kungs. In this variety of chi kung pattern, we have stationary feet while our arms move with the flow of the breath. There are many patterns of this variety, but no matter what the pattern, we have the same directive, to move the arms with the breath. The ego, of course, is quite comfortable simply taking charge of the whole thing and directing the tempo of breath and arm movement so that it looks nice and coordinated. This is the surface layer of the practice. The next step is to drop control and actually follow the breath (rather than our prejudgment of how the breath and arm movements should be).

Photo 15

We can use a simple version of this that many people will be familiar with - starting in "Holding the Moon", a weight 50-50, feet hip to shoulder width, standing meditation posture. The arms are held a little below shoulder level, palms facing the body, as if holding the moon (or a large beach ball) against the chest. The full body breathing pattern is to move the arms apart and open, broaden the back and chest on the inhale, and allow the fingers to return more to the center on the exhale. So as you inhale, the "moon" and body expand, as you exhale they deflate. (photo 15)

Be curious how to follow, rather than control the movement. Use your intent-to-follow to create a physical willingness to be moved, to create space into which your breath and chi can flow and allow your movement to express itself. Personally, I still find this a useful exercise. I am still improving my sensitivity and I still get sucked in by the desire to be in control. I find that I come closer to the moment to moment magic of my breath and movement by supporting its flow. That is, as I observe my breath and movement, I make sure that the impact of my observing is in the same direction as the natural flow. My contact with my breath and movement has an open, curious quality to it. For me, this attitude creates a profound shift in my experience.

Going with the flow requires the sensitivity to be able to perceive the flow and join with it without disrupting it. Correct intent and attitude can create a physical and energetic willingness to follow, making us more responsive. By studying the flow we can start to predict, support and influence its motion.

Taking the time to work with your personal challenges with listening, joining and following yourself can make it much easier to understand those same challenges when they show up with a partner. Putting some time in with this sort of exploration will deepen and improve your understanding of the push hands directive to stick/adhere in order to accurately listen to, join with and follow your partner's movement.

To close this chapter, here's a postural check list from the ground up:

- Feet relaxed with the weight spread and all three points (heel, big toe and little toe sides) connected to the earth. Ankles springy.

- Knee not going past the toe in a forward stance and not going too far to the right or left from directly over the foot. Bending the knee makes the joint more stable.

- Hip positioned so the thigh goes the same direction as the weighted leg. Sit into the hip joint so you are springy there as well.

- Relaxing and sinking into the floor of the pelvis (perineum). There should be a sense of spaciousness here with the braced legs making an upside down U at the crotch.

- Tail bone (coccyx) hanging down. The pelvis is not tucked under, nor is the back arched with the buttocks out. Some people like using the image of a large metal ball hanging down from the tailbone to help root them. I encourage you to keep your hip joints soft so that the pelvis can flex and extend with the breath and your movement. You may benefit from using the image of pushing from the coccyx when going forward and leading with the coccyx when shifting back.

- Lower back and waist loose and hanging. Feel the movement in the lower back with the breath.

- Use deep abdominal breathing to compress the abdominal organs into the pelvic bowl. This breathing, combined with sitting in the kua will literally lower you center of gravity to the tan tien. As you move, feel and imagine that you are moving from that area (two finger thicknesses below the navel).

- Shoulders settled down and attached to the rib cage and spine with the latissimus dorsi and rhomboids. Shoulder down to elbow up to wrist.

- Chest soft, bringing a sense of lift up the back with the breath, connecting the lift through the neck to the crown.

- CMC stressed keeping an extended beautiful lady's wrist, while the Yang long form is done "sitting the wrist". In push hands, the wrists and hands are shaped to their purpose.

- Tongue touches the roof of the mouth to close an energy circuit and help relax the jaw.

- Floating from the crown of the head. Cultivate a light and insubstantial energy at the crown. You might imagine a laser pointer line from the crown through the floor of the pelvis to the floor. This is your center line. Keep your body organized around your center line (vertical) and your tan tien (horizontal).

- Keep your facial expression and eyes soft.

- As you shift your weight back and forth, remember to follow the hip track. Keep the ankles, knees, and hips bent. Extend the rear leg to move forward, extend the front leg to move back. Keeping your legs slightly braced will naturally keep you in the hip track where the pelvis turns naturally as you shift back and forth, allowing the thighs to go in the same direction as the feet, avoiding a twist at the knee.

In moving with a partner:

- Maintain your own structure first!

- Let your eyes rest on the hollow of your partner's neck. In this way you will not be distracted by her eyes, while being able to see her gaze and her whole body with your peripheral vision.

- Stick to your partner, do not avoid or separate from her.

- Wait for her to initiate and follow her movement.

- Do not oppose or resist her movement, but by joining and following gain a superior position (arrive first).

Chapter 3

Level One Drills and Games

Now on to the drills and games themselves!

Different styles and different teachers have their own push-hands drills. Here are the ones I have found most useful in my own training and as a teacher. Although I stand on the shoulders of a variety of great teachers, errors and omissions in the following are my own!

The drills are meant to be done slowly with sensitivity. For the most part, the slower you go, the more you will learn. I have rarely had to admonish a student to speed up a drill, but I often must ask them to slow down. Still, from time to time, practice moving more quickly for a change of pace.

In general at this level, the amount of pressure in a push is determined by the person who is yielding. If you are pushing, push gently and allow the pressure to build up to the level your partner chooses. If you are being pushed, you determine the strength of the push by how quickly you yield to it. If you do not move out of the way, the pressure should build.

Traditional writing on T'ai Chi refers to "jings". This is usually translated as "energies". I generally prefer the term "skills". I will mention the jings associated with the skills and drills. For a more thorough discussion of jings, see <u>Advanced Yang Style T'ai Chi Chuan</u> by Yang, Jwing-Ming.

Push Hands Stances:

I need to say a few more things about stances before we get started. Most of the push hands drills and games in this workbook are called "fixed step" because neither partner is supposed to move his or her feet. Players stand in "bow and arrow" or forward stances with their forward feet parallel and the rear foot turned out 30' – 45'. If both partner's right or left feet are forward, this is called an "enclosed" stance (photo 16). If one player has the right forward and the other the left, this is a "mirror" stance (photo 17). (Those

Photo 16

Photo 17

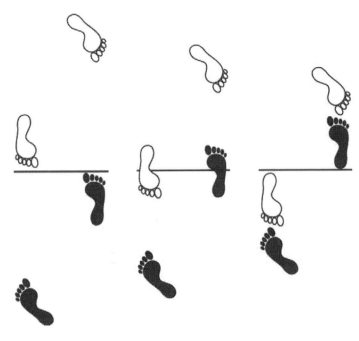

of you who are really looking at these pictures might notice that Brian is leaning a little back in these and some later pictures.. This is because he is not sitting enough in his right kua.)

In these stances, parallel lines of the forward feet are separated by 4-6 inches. As shown in figure 3, the toes can be on the same line (shallow), the toes on the same line as the partner's heel (normal), or the heels can be on the same line (deep). In practice, I often find myself standing between "shallow" and "normal", perhaps because of my long arms.

Figure 3

The length of the stance will determine how low the players go and how much movement forward and back will be possible. Lower stances require greater strength and flexibility, and can make relaxing difficult – start higher and shorter until you gain greater comfort. Working at the lower stances is good training as long as you understand that due to the strain of maintaining them, low stances may limit your mobility.

The drills are presented in the following format:

Time frame:
Focus skills:
Format:
Advanced variations:
Study questions:
Skills you must learn here in order to progress:

First level drills are concerned with developing effective stances and body structure and in connecting with your partner and perceiving him or her accurately. These skills take years to master.

Sticking Drill:

Time frame: This drill can remain useful for years. And doing it for 5 or 10 minutes will give you a taste of the challenge of sticking.

Focus skills: maintaining contact with your partner. This is to develop the sensitivity and the agility to stick to your partner's body and follow his or her movements (tsan nien jing stick/adhere).

<u>Format:</u> One partner imagines she is glued to the other partner at a physical point of contact. One partner moves, the other follows.

For example, partners might agree to be glued together at the right wrist. As the leader moves, the other must follow and maintain the point of contact. The leader may move her arm up or down at any speed and may turn and walk or run.

As the leader, be creative. Find and stretch your partner's abilities. It is not useful to move your hand so fast they can't follow, nor to run them into walls, or twist them into impossible positions.

As the follower, recognize that the exact point of contact will change angle and roll as you change position. That is fine. Just stay attached to your opponent. Rolling is fine, slipping, sliding or losing contact is not.

After a few minutes as leader, switch roles.

<u>More advanced variations:</u>
Try adhering at more difficult points – elbow, shoulder, forehead, knee, hip, back.

Try adhering to two points at once. Start with two palms and then go for different body parts – be creative.

Try connecting with two palms and leading with the right while following with the left.

Try doing this with your eyes closed. This is a technique you can use in all later drills – it allows you to focus on your sense of touch without visual input. This is a good training strategy but obviously foolish to do in real life.

<u>Study questions:</u>
What level of pressure gives you the best connection?

Are you more comfortable leading or following?

<u>Skills you must learn in this drill since they will be needed later:</u>

In working with the point of contact, there are times when you can not simply stay on the same point. When, in order to stick to your partner, you must change the point of contact, there are some ways of doing so that maintain connection and some that break it.

Generally, sliding or breaking and reaquiring the point do not maintain contact and are errors. This error is also called "discarding". In sliding we slide skin to skin. This feels a little sandpapery and is due to a loss of stable contact. Breaking and reaquiring the point is sliding made a bit worse, where we actually lose contact and then must reestablish it.

On the other hand, well executed rolling or replacing the point can keep connection even as we adjust the point. Rolling occurs naturally as we start wrist to wrist and then move – the point may roll from the inside to the outside of the wrist while still never actually breaking contact or sliding. When rolling doesn't do it and sliding or breaking are imminent, we can replace the contact by establishing a new point some where else (that does not disrupt the momentum and structure). This is a little like how you might keep your distance from a boulder, hand over hand, as you inner tube down a river.

Weight   Shifting   Drill:

<u>Time frame:</u> This drill focuses on a skill that should also be developed in your solo form practice. If you have done this, it should only take you about 10 or 20 five minute sessions to strengthen this skill enough to be able to keep it in place while doing more complicated drills.

<u>Focus skills:</u> Coordinated shifting of the weight back and forth on the hip track so that you can move with confidence and authority in either direction.

<u>Format:</u> Both standing in an enclosed stance, one person pushes the other person back with both hands. The person being pushed can have his/her arms crossed, palms on shoulders, to provide a solid structure to receive the push. As you are pushed, resist enough with the rear leg so that the pusher must compress your leg for you. Following the hip track, allow the pelvis, navel, shoulder girdle and nose to turn to the side the rear foot is facing. As you receive the push, feel your partner compressing you into Kidney One (K1) at the ball of your rear foot (photo 18)

In Wu style push hands, as you shift back, the front toe rises. Generally in Yang style this is seen as an error. The broad minded may choose to experiment. My view is that if the toe is raised with tension, this is an error. If your stability is undermined by raising the toe, this is also an error. On the other hand, the same statements are true for not raising the toe. The important thing is to shift back into a position that is comfortable, balanced and strong.

Photo 18

Once you are fully back let your partner know and shift forward so he or she can push you again.

If you are pushing, move forward and back by pushing from one leg into the other. Make sure your pelvis follows the hip track and allow your legs, not your arms, to do the pushing. Keep the angles at the elbows greater than 90'.

<u>More advanced variations</u>:

<u>Pull instead of pushing</u> (photo 19) Some people perceive this skill more easily with a pull than a push. To set this up, use the same right sided forward stance and grip left wrists. Make sure your grip is strong, extend your arm a little so the scapula is away from the spine and also sunken with the lat.

Then one person pulls strongly and steadily on the other. Use your legs to pull and also your legs to resist being pulled. The arms do not move much. Push out of the front leg to pull and brace into the front leg to resist. The legs are stronger than the arms, so do not resist as strongly as you can lest you strain your shoulder. The person being pulled is in charge of how much he resists, and thus how much strain to endure. Do not jerk. Do not try to pull your partner over. Focus on connecting the pull of your legs into your arm and connecting through the balls of the feet into the earth. Then switch roles.

Photo 19

<u>Take the push on the shoulders.</u>
(photo 20) One person is pushed on both shoulders. Yield to it. As you approach the end of your range to the rear, bring your hands up your midline and brush them outwards close to your shoulders to remove (shrug off) your partner's hands. Do not separate your hands farther than necessary to neutralize before switching to yang. Now come in to push back. When you are pushing, test your partner by stopping pushing. Do not retreat until you are pushed back (stick to your partner's push)!

<u>Treat the push as a two hand choke to the neck.</u>
(photo 21) Move slowly and carefully to avoid injury! As your partner reaches for

Photo 20

your neck, retreat just in front of his attack. As you shift into the rear leg, control his hands with your rear hand and forward forearm and counter to his neck or eyes with your forward hand (as Brian is doing to me). Feel the forward foot free to kick or step. Release you counter and switch roles.

Photo 21

<u>Take the push on the crest of your hips.</u> (photo 22) Again, yield to it and make sure to turn your pelvis as you retreat. As you reach your rear limit, bring your hands down at your midline to brush your partner's hands off (as Brian is doing) and then come forward to push back.

<u>Study questions</u>:
How strongly do your legs need to be braced (pushing against one another) to ensure that you follow the hip track?

How much pressure can you take at the shoulder level before your back starts to arch?

How can you adjust your body to accommodate the pressure from the front and not allow your back to become vulnerable?

<u>Skills you must learn here in order to progress:</u>

Photo 22

You must be able to follow the hip track forward or back under pressure. This pressure may be physical or emotional. The waist must be protected by properly setting the body up to receive a load from the front. Many teachers refer to this as "tucking the tailbone under" since the back becomes vulnerable by the opposite, arching. Do not "tuck" with tension.

Arching the back is generally an error although a small amount may be necessary at times to assist with "shrugging off" an attack to shoulder level.

Wrist and Elbow Joint Circles:

This is a solo drill for building the physical coordination required for the skillful rotation of these joints around the point of contact. It is also great for range of motion and massage of the joints.

<u>Time frame:</u> This focuses on a coordination skill that will take ten minutes to understand and a few hours to have down. The wrist skill is used in the next partner drill and the elbow skill first in single handed circling. Once you have the feel of this, keep it in your repertoire as a wrist and elbow range of motion drill.

<u>Focus skills:</u> Besides the obvious coordination development, this drill is a good solo method to study the issue of sticking and rolling the point.

<u>Format:</u> Try it first at the elbow. Put the left palm on the outside of the right elbow. The pressure of the left palm is the point of contact.

Draw a continuing circle with the right fingers pointing diagonally to the left, going up inside the left arm, close to the body and down outside the left arm, further from the body.

Or to describe the elbow, move the right forearm so that the point of contact goes over the top of the elbow, down the outside, under the bottom and up the inside.

Or to describe it as an elbow massage, circle the left palm around the right elbow joint pressing chi into the joint first over the top of the elbow, down the outside, under the bottom and up the inside. Move the right forearm to allow this.

Got it? Now reverse. And then do it in both directions on the other side.

This kind of circling may occur when the forward motion of the arm is blocked at the elbow. Notice that if the elbow is blocked (or connected to your partner's elbow), this circle allows either a back fist to the face or a hammer fist to the groin.

Try this same drill with the wrist. Put the left palm against the back of the right wrist and press. This is the point of contact.

Draw a continuing circle with the right fingers pointing diagonally to the left, going up inside the left arm, close to the body and down outside the left arm, further from the body.

Or to describe the motion at the wrist, move the right hand so that the point of contact goes over the top of the wrist, down the outside, under the bottom and up the inside.

Or to describe it as a wrists massage, circle the left palm around the right wrist pressing chi into the joint first over the top of the wrist, down the outside, under the bottom and up the inside. Move the right hand to allow this.

Now reverse. And then do it in both directions on the other side.

This kind of circling may occur when the forward motion of the hand is blocked at the wrist, or when you want to circle from one side to the other of your partner's hand.

Sticking   with   Wrists:

This is a cooperative Chen style drill for sticking.

<u>Time frame:</u> This drill can remain useful for years. Doing it for three 10 minute sessions should make it obvious that more practice will lead to improvement.

<u>Focus skills:</u> maintaining contact with your partner. This is to develop the sensitivity and the agility to stick to your partner's body and follow his or her movements especially with the arms (tsan nien jing stick/adhere).

<u>Format:</u> There are three types of these. For each, both stand in an enclosed stance. Keep the tempo easy so that the movement is fluid and relaxing. These are great for your rotator cuffs at the shoulder.

1) Connect at the wrists with one person (A, Nando in the photos) beneath the wrists of the other (B, Brian). A leads, maintaining more control over B's wrists. B follows and sticks. Stay connected at the wrists. A shifts forward and raises his and B's wrists up B's midline (photo 23). A shifts back and separates both his and his partner's arms out and down (photo 24). A shifts forward again and raises his and B's wrists up B's midline.

Photo 23

Photo 24

Then reverse roles and directions. B leads, maintaining more control over A's wrists. A follows and sticks.

• B shifts forward pushing his and A's wrists back towards A's hips.
• B starts to shift back and separates both his arms and moves his wrists up.
• A reaches towards B's head with both hands (as in Two Winds to the Ears in the solo form).
• B drapes his wrists over A's and pushes them down his midline and shifts forward pushing his and A's wrists back towards A's hips.

Switching roles gives two more variations, so there are four versions of this with each leg forward for a total of eight variations. Do them each for a minute each practice session.

2) Connect at the wrists with each person's wrists to his right of his partner's. A initiates, but partners cooperate to keep sticking. A moves the arms, stuck at the wrists, in a clockwise (CW) or counter clockwise (C-CW) circle on a vertical plane. Start with no weight shift, and then add the weight shift. It is easiest if you shift forward as the circle moves to your right (either high (CW) or low (C-CW), but it can be done the other way also (photos 25,26).

Photo 25

Photo 26

Once you can do it this way, switch roles so that B initiates. Then move your wrists to your left of your partner's. Take turns initiating in both directions. Then do the same with the other foot forward. That is 16 variations! Do them each for thirty seconds each session.

3) If you change the timing of the first version, you can create an eggbeater kind of motion. The hands either move up or down the midline, and one pair goes first, then the next. Partners cooperate to create the pattern. A for instance, could initiate doing a CW circle with his right and a C-CW circle with his left. As you experiment, remember to move your arms from your legs and waist, not from your shoulders. Keep the movement at a tempo where you can coordinate the arm motion and your weight shift and waist turn.

Skills you must learn in this drill:

This drill builds on the first sticking drill and adds the weight shift and more cooperative flow. It's essential that you follow the hip track in your weight shift. The flow of the movement will help you loosen your arms and further develop your skills of rolling the point. Be attentive to preventing the errors of sliding or breaking contact. If you find your arms feeling tight or clumsy in later drills, this is a good one to come back to in order to loosen up. Aspects of the third, freer style will show up in later drills.

Twisting Around the Center Line Drill:

Time frame: This drill will take only a moment to understand, but will remain useful for training flexibility and listening for many hours. You can use this as a warm up at the start of a push hands session.

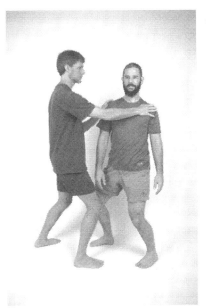

Focus skills: maintaining your body upright under pressure and sensing (ting jing or listening) and yielding to a push by twisting (hua jing or neutralizing).

Format: (photos 27, 28) Both stand in an enclosed stance. One person pushes 4 times, then switch. The pushes are linear pushes delivered with one hand at a time to shoulder or hip. The person being pushed can have his/her arms crossed, palms on shoulders, to provide a solid structure to receive the push and protect her breasts.

Photo 27   Photo 28

The person being pushed twists around his midline to spin off the push. This may require shifting the weight back or forward. Do not sacrifice your leg and pelvis structure or your body upright to twist! Do not require yourself to back up in order to spin off the push. Sometimes you can improve your position by spinning a push off while going forward.

As much as possible, allow your partner to move you, do not help him. If you shift back, do so because he is compressing you into your rear leg. If you spin, do so because he provides the energy for the motion. At first, you will need to allow your partner's pressure to build a certain amount to perceive its direction. As you become more perceptive and your body's movement more fluid, you will need less pressure.

When pushing, pay attention to your own leg, pelvis structure and body upright to provide a strong linear push.

Pushes are easier to yield to the further out from the center line they are, so start pushing on shoulders or hips and move closer to the center as your partner becomes more experienced. Similarly, linear pushes are easier to yield to than pushes that follow you as you twist. So start with clear linear pushes, then graduate to following your partner as (s)he turns.

Always push slowly and gently and do not poke. The pusher should work on her sensitivity to pushing as the person being pushed works on his sensitivity to the push. As you become familiar with yielding to the push by shifting back and turning, you can invite your partner to push closer to your centerline. Maintain your body upright and keep your stance strong. Note that as the pushes move closer to the midline, they become more difficult to spin off and, inevitably, we will get pushed out of our stance. Don't fret about it! It's only a drill. Keep your attention on developing your responsiveness to the push and being able to precisely discern its direction.

Advanced variations:

Do not allow yourself to move back or forward. Receive the pushes with your weight 100% back, 90%, 70%, 50%, 30%, 10% and 100% forward. Test your range of motion, being careful to maintain your leg, pelvis structure and body upright.

As the pusher, make the vector of your pushes go upwards or downwards as opposed to simply horizontal.

When you are being pushed, close your eyes. Your partner is free to move around you and push you in any direction at will. Keep the pushes slow and gentle - no poking.

As the pusher, keep your partner back on his rear leg and get him to twist back and forth around his centerline while remaining stable on his leg. When he tires, it is your turn!

Study questions:
How does the amount of pressure required to push you back compare with the amount required to cause you to spin? How does the musculature involved differ?

How do these interact when the push is more complicated?

How exactly do you discern the direction of a push?
What is required to make the process of yielding to the push integral to the process of perceiving its direction?

<u>Skills you must learn here in order to progress:</u>

You must be able to distinguish between shifting back and spinning to yield to a push and be able to integrate them effectively in three dimensions. You must be able to generate a push effectively with the forward or rear hand.

Neutralizing:

Neutralizing (hua jing) usually involves spinning around one's center and is often combined with yielding – shifting back. As I've mentioned, beach balls are experts at neutralizing – push one down into a pool and it will spin around your push to come up to the surface. As demonstrated by the beach ball, neutralizing does not require a cerebral cortex! The more you are able to allow your body to simply respond to the push without thought, the more effectively you will neutralize.

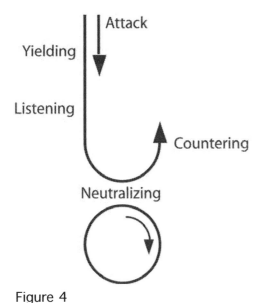

Figure 4

As shown in figure 4, as the attack comes in, align with it by yielding and listening. Then neutralize by turning around your center, then counter.

The beach ball neutralizes and comes up to the surface. When you receive a push, neutralize and come forward with your counter. When you are pushed, you may choose to yield. The purpose of yielding is to:
- Get enough information so that you understand your partner's push and perceive his center
- Allow your partner to express his energy so that it weakens
- Absorb some of the push so that you can borrow its energy

If you do not need to yield in order to do this, neutralizing immediately is appropriate.

Another image for this is where we imagine the push as a rock tossed into a pond, the water allows the rock to pass while splashing up around the edges. When the push comes in, neutralize the push and counter around its edge.

Neutralizing usually requires turning. The turn should be initiated at your center and manifest in the torso and arms. It often involves opening and closing at the kua. The plane of the turn can be at any angle. This skill is developed by making big circles at first and gradually being able to make them smaller. Skilled practitioners can neutralize immediately with little perceptible movement.

If you do not effectively neutralize, you will find yourself pushing back against your partner's push. The substance of your partner's push is felt as hard and solid, the edge is where that hardness turns soft and empty. As shown in figure 5, counter there! As with the rock tossed into the pond image, your counter is most effective right at the edge of the hardness of the attack. Challenge yourself to perceive this edge and to develop the finesse to push there.

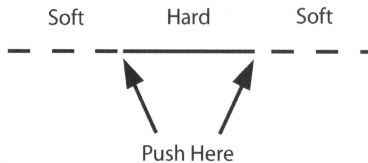

Figure 5

Finding Your Root:

<u>Focus skills:</u> Understanding and strengthening your balance.

In T'ai Chi, people often talk about the "root" in language that does not really help beginners. It <u>is</u> useful to visualize the soles of the feet opening and connecting through energetic roots with the earth at the bubbling well (Kidney 1). But let's start with a more pragmatic approach.

Balance is primarily a strength, perception and coordination issue. Assuming that your inner ears work (the perception part), pay attention to your sense of support through the standing leg and adjust as necessary to maximize it. Feel the contact between your foot and the ground. At minimum, be aware of the three points of each foot – heel, little toe and big toe side - and make sure that each is in contact with the floor. Make sure your weight is going through the center of the ankle, that there is no twist in the knee and that the hip joint is loose.

Standing stationery is a great laboratory to study and strengthen your root, but recognize that your real target is to be able to step from one rooted position swiftly into another. A great deal of this skill comes from being so familiar with the structure and alignment of your support (which usually needs some sense of bracing your legs) that you naturally settle into this position after moving a foot.

As a **solo exploration**, put your feet together, knees soft, and move the hands to the left and right like a hula dancer. Counter-balancing at the hips should happen spontaneously. Move the arms forward and then back, again the hips should counter-balance spontaneously, bending at the knee and sticking the bottom out as the hands go forward (photo 29), arching in the back a bit as the arms go back. Do this until your body learns to allow the counter-balance to occur by itself.

In the solo form, when we take a step, there is always a counter-balancing arm motion. Find them and make sure you are using/allowing them.

In two person drills, we often keep ourselves stable by counter-balancing. I once got to push with David Leung of Eugene, Oregon who is so good at this that he can go up on his toes and bend back at his knees as if doing the limbo. I could actually push down on him in this position and he was springy! Excellent counter-balancing!

Sometimes you may find yourself grabbing on to your partner in order to keep from falling over. This is using them as a counter-balance and in a fight may be better than falling over, but is a potentially confusing move in training. Even if by grabbing you are able to keep your feet and dislodge your partner, you are the one who first lost your balance. To keep yourself honest, see grabbing as an error.

Photo 29

Photo 30

Standing meditations are great practices for studying and strengthening balance. Most serious T'ai Chi players practice standing regularly. You will experience the benefits if you practice for a week aiming for ten minutes a day. If you get tired, stop and walk around a bit to rest.

Here are four standing postures, treat the descriptions as a guide and find the nuances that personalize these stances.

Wu Chi: (photo 30) Stand with the feet parallel, hip width apart, arms at sides, palms facing the rear. Scan from the crown of the head down to the soles of your feet relaxing and opening the joints. Floating from the crown of the head, tongue touching the roof of the mouth, chin dropped, neck free, shoulder blades sinking and widening, space under the arm pits, arms and hands alive to the finger tips, breathing deeply into the pelvic bowl, feel and open the perineum, hip joints loose, weight going down the center of loose knees and ankles, feeling the bubbling wells. Whole body mobile with the breath - allow the pelvis to move with the breath. (For more discussion on this important relationship, see the article on learning to relax in the appendix.) Expect, feel and allow the subtle balance adjustments and sway that go with the pulse of the breath and simply standing. The dance of the standing body is like the movement of a flame around the wick of a candle on a windless night. Bracing your legs will increase the work done in this stance and reduce the sway.

If you find yourself mentally drifting, bring your attention back to your present tense physical sensations and perceptions.

Holding the moon: (photo 31) Stand with the feet parallel or turned in just a bit, slightly wider than hip width apart, arms horizontally in front of you holding an imaginary ball with the palms facing the chest. Shoulder down to elbow up to finger tips, allow the ball to expand and contract a bit with the breath to keep the arms and shoulders relaxed. Scan from the crown of the head down to the soles of the feet relaxing and opening the joints. Floating from the crown of the head, tongue touching the roof of the mouth, chin dropped, neck free, shoulder blades sinking and widening, arms and hands alive to the finger tips, breathing deeply into the pelvic bowl, feel and open the perineum, hip joints loose, weight going down the center of loose knees and ankles, feeling the bubbling wells. Whole body mobile with the breath - feel and allow the subtle balance adjustments that go with the pulse of the breath and simply standing. If you find yourself drifting away, bring your attention back to present tense physical sensations and perceptions.

Photo 31

Universal post: (photo 32) Standing with 99% of the weight in one leg the other foot at rest slightly forward and to the side, arms horizontally in front of you holding an imaginary ball with the palms facing the chest. Shoulder down to elbow up to finger tips, allow the ball to expand and contract a bit with the breath to keep the arms and shoulders relaxed. Breathe especially deeply into the weighted hip joint to keep this area relaxed and mobile (flexing and extending slightly with the breath). Scan from the crown of the head down to the soles of the feet relaxing and opening the joints. Floating from the crown of the head, tongue touching the roof of the mouth, chin dropped, neck free, shoulder blades sinking and widening, arms and hands alive to the finger tips, breathing deeply into the pelvic bowl, feel and open the perineum, hip joint loose, weight going down the center of the untwisted weighted knee and ankle, feeling the bubbling well. Whole body mobile with the breath. Feel and allow the subtle balance adjustments

Photo 32

that go with the pulse of the breath and simply standing. If you find yourself drifting away, simply bring your attention back to present tense physical sensations and perceptions.

Photo 33

San ti: (photo 33) Standing with 90% of the weight in one leg, the other foot at rest slightly forward and to the side, arms in front of you with arms mirroring the position of the legs. The imaginary ball is more the shape of a large zucchini with the palms facing a little downward. Shoulder down to elbow up to finger tips, (some people sit the wrists) allow the chest to expand and contract with the breath to keep the arms and shoulders relaxed. Breathe especially deeply into the weighted hip joint to keep this area relaxed and mobile (flexing and extending slightly with the breath). Scan from the crown of the head down to the soles of the feet relaxing and opening the joints. Floating from the crown of the head, tongue touching the roof of the mouth, chin dropped, neck free, shoulder blades sinking and widening, arms and hands alive to the finger tips, breathing deeply into the pelvic bowl, feel and open the perineum, hip joint loose, weight going down the center of the untwisted weighted knee and ankle, feeling the bubbling well. Whole body mobile with the breath. Feel and allow the subtle balance adjustments that go with the pulse of the breath and simply standing. If you find yourself drifting away, simply bring your attention back to present tense physical sensations and perceptions.

Regular practice of these and other standing postures will strengthen your legs and your connection to the earth.

Brace the legs, but not too much.   As I mentioned earlier, bracing the legs as if on board a rocking ship or train will make you more stable. The leg muscles are used to place the bones in a position where they can absorb shock well. At first you will probably brace too hard, using more muscular force than is ultimately necessary. This is tiring and may create some initial soreness in your leg muscles. Expect this and allow yourself to ease off on the tension used over time. Too much bracing makes the whole body stiff and limits your freedom of motion. Too little makes you flaccid and easily dislodged.

Some practitioners avoid the term, "bracing", because there is such potential misunderstanding it as "bracing to receive a blow" which usually is a fearful stiffening of the whole body. This is not what I mean and I look forward to finding a phrase that avoids this potential misunderstanding. You might prefer the term "structure".

What I mean by bracing is to place the bones such that the joints are most able to respond to shocks. Try to find the minimum amount of tone required to give you a good structure. This structure is required in order to transmit the solidity of the earth through your legs and pelvis. This same isometric approach is used to further transmit this solidity through the waist, chest and arms to create resilient peng or ward off energy. If you will recall, all movements in the form are supposed to have peng, so my hope is that you have been practicing this for some time. If not, start now! Use these push hands drills to test and challenge your peng strength. For further discussion of this, see Sigman's internet writings.

Immoveable Ward Off:

Time frame: This drill focuses on the skill of correct body placement. It will take only moments to discover that certain structures work and others do not. Having discovered this, it then takes practice to dwell in functional structures at all times. Your form should be a place of solo practice for this, but periodic external verification remains useful for years. Once you have a good feel of this, that testing will occur within later drills and games.

Focus skills: Organizing your structure to be able to receive horizontal pressure with either the forward or back arm.

Format: Both stand in an enclosed stance. One person pushes with a hand on the other's elbow and wrist. The other person receives the push without moving (photos 34,35).

When you are pushing, build the pressure up slowly and direct it through your partner's center towards the rear foot. The point is to give your partner the opportunity and time to find her root, not to push him over. Once your partner is able to receive you, push more strongly towards his rear foot. When you are receiving, extend from your rear foot, through your waist, towards the push. Position your back to avoid arching.

To receive with the forward arm (photo 34), allow the navel to be turned slightly to the inside. To receive with the rear arm (photo 35), close the front kua and turn the navel a bit to the outside. In both cases, keep the angle at the elbow greater than 90' and keep the elbow low.

Photo 34

Photo 35

Advanced variations:

As you receive the push, the weight from the forward leg will be taken up by your partner's push until it is empty. Notice this point and as soon as you are able, lift your foot (without disturbing your balance or alerting your partner) to prove to yourself that you can. You will use this skill in moving step drills.

Once you can receive pressure directed towards your rear foot, have your partner simply push horizontally. Modify your own structure to direct it to the rear foot. Allow yourself to twist a little around the mid line and adjust the pelvis, waist and weight if appropriate to channel the push down into your rear leg..

Study questions:
Experiment with arm angles as you receive. Do it wrong on purpose. How much can you vary your position before the structure breaks down?

Do the same thing with your initial weight distribution.

Do the same thing with the angle of the navel.

Do the same thing with the structure of the spine.

A few more variations:
As your ability to channel your partner's push down to the earth and your sense of root improves, experiment with receiving pushes from the sides and the back. Notice that it is very difficult to be stable when your partner pushes towards the quadrants where you do not have a leg to brace with.

You can also experiment with pulling your partner. Try pulling on a knee, thigh, arm or shoulder. Pushes get grounded into the rear leg, pulls down into the front leg. As you are being pulled, notice how you could let go and barrel right into your partner. Pulls are only wise if you are sure your partner isn't going to use it as an invitation to fall into you with an elbow!

Once you have these down you can further test your stability by standing on bricks. Use regular red masonry bricks, one under each foot. Start with them on the largest side, then the smaller and then on end. Each partner stands on bricks. This is hard, but forces you to pay attention to the contact of your foot through the brick to the ground. It will strengthen your whole leg structure over time. This looks bizarre enough to convince everyone that you are a serious martial artist!

Skills you must learn here in order to progress:
You must have choice (within the limits of your structure) about whether to retreat or not. This requires that you be familiar with precisely how to use your body to be ready to receive horizontal force.

In the game of push hands, calmly receiving your partner's force and directing it down into your rear foot can be very useful. In free sparring, being able to move and instantly establish a solid structure can make the difference between being safe and being hit.

From these drills, you should now have the skills you need to play the first push hands game. Congratulations!

Free Form Game 1: Seeking Center

This game combines the skills you have developed by spending time on these first several drills. In the drills you have been pushing in lines, like taking aim and shooting an arrow. For this

game, push as if trying to keep an inflated ball underwater - as you push the ball down it will roll and spin to come up - to keep it under you will need to compensate. Similarly, as your partner shifts and turns to yield to your push, readjust to continue pushing through her center.

Focus skills: Sensing and adhering to your partner's center. Remaining flexible and elusive as your partner pursues your center. Neutralizing in order to change from yin, receptive, to yang, assertive.

Format: (photo 36, 37) Both stand in an enclosed stance. One person pushes slowly and persistently towards the other's center, modifying his push as his partner yields. Push with both hands on whatever your partner gives you to push on. The other shifts back, twists around the midline or settles into an "immovable" structure, playing with creative ways to elude the push and oppor-

Photo 36

tunities to turn the tables and push back. Go back and forth, maintaining good leg, hip structure and your body upright. This game is best done quite slowly with sensitivity, but also try it faster for more dynamic fun.

You may find yourself pushing on your partner's arms, shoulders, hips or chest. Generally it is best when being pushed to receive the push on your arms. Once your partner's hand is on your torso, he could strike your internal organs. It is better to keep an extra layer of protection up - maintain your ward off and keep your partner's hands off your body.

Photo 37

<u>Little tricks</u>:

As you are pushed, settle into "immovability" to get your partner to commit and then swiftly change and yield to knock him off.

When you push, always push towards the quadrant where your partner's legs are not (his open door). When receiving, always receive into a leg.

If you have the opportunity, experiment with pulling your partner towards his forward open door.

Remember: be playful, laugh and have fun!

<u>To close this chapter, recall these points for moving with a partner:</u>

- Maintain your own structure first! Preserve the ability to spin on your center line by keeping your vertical extension and alignment as you shift your weight back and forth.

- Let your eyes rest on the hollow of your partner's neck. In this way you will not be distracted by her eyes, while being able to see her gaze and her whole body with your peripheral vision.

- Stick to your partner, do not avoid or separate from her. Direct your attention through the point of contact to your partner's center.

- Wait for her to initiate and follow her movement.

- Do not oppose or resist her movement, but by joining and following gain a superior position (arrive first).

- Push at the edges of your partner's solidity, like stream water flowing around a rock.

- When pushed, receive it first. Extend from the earth, through your center to the point of contact. Then yield first with the legs, then with the arms and if necessary, with the body.

Chapter 4

Understanding the Process of Pushing:

Generally in push hands instruction the bulk of attention is paid to the skills of dealing with a push. This makes sense since T'ai Chi is a defensive, rather than an offensive art. Still, in order to be skilled in push hands and have the most fun, you need to work on your offensive game as well.

The power of a push should come from your legs, be directed by the angle of your pelvis and waist and be manifested through your arms and hands. It is possible to push horizontally, up, down and to either side. Your push can manifest through either or both hands. For that matter, it can also manifest through any other part of your body. It can be very short (more like a strike), or long (as in pushing away). It can be fast or slow, superficial or deep.

In order to push effectively, you need to be able to perceive your partner's center. This requires sensitivity, which, as we have discussed above, requires relaxation. So when we push, we want the body to remain supple and soft. Generally, we would like our push to be set up so that the force comes from pushing against the ground, through our center, to our arms and hands, into our partner's body, through their center and knocks them over. If we miss their center, we might well find ourselves in the dirt.

To return to our simile, a skillful partner is like a beach ball we are trying to push under water. She will spin, retreat and try to slip by us to counter, and our push must remain on her center despite her changes to be effective.

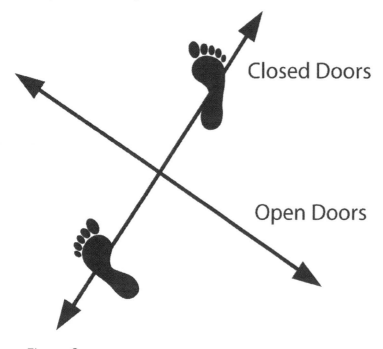

Closed Doors

Open Doors

Figure 6

Perceiving Your Partner's Center:

As you push your partner, he will try to yield and evade by turning on his center line. If you push high or low, he will yield in an arc that goes around his center horizontally as well. Use his changes to triangulate on your target. Once you have a feel for his center's location, push it or pull it towards one of the quadrants with no leg (an "open door" in figure 6). If instead you push his center into his rear leg (a "closed door"), he may simply be able to root against your push and borrow your force to overcome you.

Whenever you push towards your partner, you should generally be either trying to locate, lock up or push on your partner's center.

When you push your partner you will have the following four experiences:
<u>Your partner feels solid</u> either because he can root your push or because he is using force against your force.
<u>Your partner feels soft</u> either because he can yield to your push or because he has no support behind that area and is about to fall over.

The trick is to be able to discern what these experiences mean, since each has a 50/50 chance of being a good sign!

Generally, when your partner is able to root your push you can look at what is happening and see that you are pushing into his rear leg. He feels solid and springy.

When your partner is using force against force, he is straining and has a more brittle, tense and shakey feel. If you can root his force at this time and coax him gently to an open door, he will fall through it. Sometimes you will not be able to do that and his strength will overpower your push. Then the thing to do is simply to shift to yin and yield. Usually people use force against force out of ignorance (they do not know that this is not what we want to be practicing here, or they are unaware that they are doing it) or out of fear. If you can find a way to discuss it kindly, you will be doing your partner a great service.

Generally when your partner feels soft because he is effectively yielding to your push, he is turning, rolling or slipping your push. This is the softness of having your push neutralized. His movement is three dimensionally complex. If he is effective, he is just about to finish neutralizing and push you.

On the other hand, when you are pushing your partner over through his open door, he feels soft because he is falling or crumpling. His movement is simple. And satisfying (to you, at least)!

Here's an exploration to get a feel for these differences.
Facing each other in a right sided enclosed stance, set up a two handed push at the wrist and elbow of your partner's right ward off.

- Push him back into his rear leg so he can root. Stay there for a moment with him comfortable and feel his solidity.

- Push him back towards a point a foot to his right of his rear foot (an open door). Have him struggle to stay upright by using force against or across your push. Hold that position for a moment to listen to the quality of vibration in his body that tells you he is straining. Can you see Brian straining in photo 38?

- Push him back towards a point behind his right shoulder (when his weight is forward). Feel the quality of softness in his yield and the complexity of the movement. Notice that as he neutralizes he is acquiring a superior position.

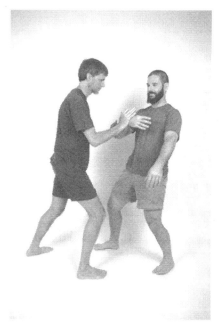

- Push him back towards his rear leg and when he is half way back change your direction to push towards his open door. Unless he struggles (force against force) he will remain soft until he falls over.

- Now switch roles so he can feel these four qualities in you.

Understanding "Double Weighting":

Double weighting is an error that is mentioned several times in the Classics. It is described as a fault in form practice and in push hands. It is usually described as
1) Having your weight evenly distributed on both feet
2) Having a push coming equally from both hands
3) Trying to push from the hand that is on the same side as the weighted leg.

Photo 38

To me these are three different kinds of faults and merit independent names and discussion.

#1) In form practice, in the beginning and end you settle into a posture where the weight is evenly distributed from one foot to the other. This is correct. As you shift your weight forward and back, you pass through a moment when the weight is 50/50. This is correct. If you root to receive a push from the front with your weight forward, as the push builds, you pass through a moment when the weight is 50/50. This is correct. If you yield to a push going from forward to back, you pass through a moment when the weight is 50/50. This is correct.

However, if you remain in a 50/50 position when pushing or you seek it as a stable posture in which to receive a push, this is incorrect. The 50/50 position tends to expose your open doors and thus is a poor posture for both pushing and receiving.

A refinement of this double weighting concept is to apply it to feet or hands. Your foot and leg is most agile if most of the weight is forward (on the ball) as opposed to evenly distributed (flat footed). The hand is most agile if the push is clearly in one quadrant formed by the two axes of top/bottom and right/left (figure 7).

Figure 7

2) Since a strong push passes through your center, pushing with the right hand requires that the push start from the left foot and vice versa. Thus, if you push equally with both arms, this will support double weighting in the legs.

3) Finally, trying to push with the same side hand as the weighted leg either creates a reliance on strength or tends to spin the body around the weighted leg (photo 39). Neither of these is good. Be clear that when you push with the right hand in a right foot forward stance, the push should be coming from the extension of the left leg (photo 40). If you start a push with your right from a position where your weight is forward already, the only source of power is your arm strength or a twist down your right leg.

Photo 39

Photo 40

Both of these might work, but we do not want to train either of them because they are fundamentally weak. On the other hand, with your weight already forward, a push with the left hand can root through your right leg and make use of the closing of the right kua for power.

Experiment with these pushes with a partner to clearly understand the weakness of double weighting.

Understanding Vectors:

"Vectors" are a method used in physics to describe the strength and direction of a force. In understanding pushing, we need to be able to talk about both of these. Vectors can be represented on paper by drawing arrows of specific length going in specific directions. One of the most important aspects of vectors to our discussion is that they can be added.

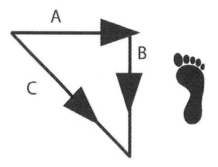

Looking at figure 8, this means that if you have your right foot forward, my push of four pounds to your rear (B, with my right) combined with a pull of three pounds to your right (A, with my left) combines to make a five pound push through your open door (C). Try it! As you can see in photos 41 and 42, it is very effective.

Figure 8

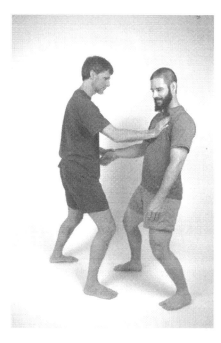

The above discussion about double weighting may have made you hesitant to push with both hands, yet it is through the perceptive combination of vectors that we can triangulate through our partner's center. One hand is the stronger pushing hand, while the other fine tunes the push, locking your partner's center up and making the push complex and responsive enough so that it is difficult to evade.

Photo 41   Photo 42

Often pushing a little up or down with the tuning hand can make a push much more difficult to neutralize. The tuning hand should be supported through the extension of the opposite leg just as is the primary pushing hand.

Exploration: Set up in standard same side, two hand push hands structure. One person pushes on elbow and wrist. With the right foot forward and the right arm in ward off, the pushing hand is on the wrist and the tuning hand is at the elbow. As you push your partner back with your right hand, aim the push through her open door with your left (by easing her to your left and taking any pivoting she does to her right horizontally through your body to augment the push with your right).

Play with this on both sides in both roles.

In a more free-form structure, with the right arm on the left and the left arm on the right, push to her center with your right while pivoting counter clockwise. Connect your pivot through both arms to her center – left arm drawing out, right arm pushing through.

These two experiments should give you ideas to explore more deeply.

The Error of Force Against Force:

When we use force against force we are committing the error of using li, heavy strength. This is also called opposing. Some pressure at the point of contact is necessary in order to perceive the incoming force and to align your structure to respond. As your skill increases, the amount of pressure needed should decrease.

As discussed earlier, the pressure at the point of contact is primarily determined by the person who is yielding. Responsive yielding should lead to little pressure at the point of contact. When you are yielding, pay attention to this so that you do not use force against your partner's push.

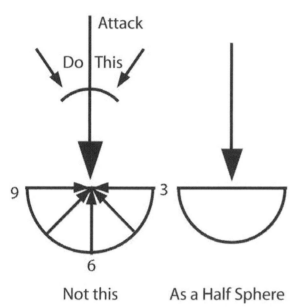

If we represent the incoming force as a vector going to 6 o'clock, any force that you apply going from 9 to 6 to 3 will be against that force as illustrated on the left in figure 9. Instead, your deflecting 4 ounces should be within 45' of the incoming force.

Although I am describing this as a two dimensional issue, there is really a half sphere of directions from which your force can come that will be against the incoming force and a cone 45' around the incoming vector that will not be force against force.

This is important to really understand, so read this again if you need to!

Figure 9

This issue applies to receiving a push, and to pushing as well. As discussed above, when you are pushing and you encounter resistance, your partner is either struggling or rooting. Either way, continuing to push on his resistance is using force against force in pushing. If you are strong you may well "win" but this will not train the skills you seek.

Instead, when you encounter a sense of solidity in your partner, think of your push as water going around a rock. Seek the edge of his solidity and slip around it to push him into emptiness. Understand his open doors and push or pull him towards one. Use the combined pushes from the primary and tuning hands to make your push complex.

The Error of Leaning:

In doing push hands, if you are relying on your partner for your balance, this is called leaning. If I lean on my partner, he controls my balance as Brian does in photo 43. Good for him, not good for me. If on the other hand, I can entice my partner to overextend himself, he will lean on me or fall over. Good for me, not so good for him.

Leaning can occur at the very beginning of play at the moment of contact. Stay on your own side of the point of contact at all times! Rely on your own balance, staying over you own feet, and within your own limits. If your partner suddenly disappeared during your play, you should not fall over.

A good exploration for this is to stand at the initial point of contact and practice each being on your own side, and then each in turn leaning on the other. This can be pretty subtle and by doing things wrong on purpose we are often more able to perceive how to do them right.

If you are bigger or stronger than your partner, it may be tempting to overpower him by leaning. Don't. Invest in loss and train your structure and sensitivity.

Photo 43

When you push with someone who leans, his touch will feel heavy and trapping. This is a result of him grounding into the earth through your body. The best thing that you can do for a partner like this is to discuss it and ask him to stop. Unfortunately, leaning is often a habitual and pervasive pattern in a person's life, so your partner may not know how to stop. Interpersonally this usually shows up as a desire to control others – wanting other people to be a certain way so that you are comfortable. This is leaning on someone else to keep your center. Your most powerful gift to someone like this may be to entice him to lean on you even more and then drop him. Repeatedly. "Do not hang your meat on my body!" – Yang, Cheng Fu

If you feel or think that your partner is leaning, make a rapid change – take the part of your body he is leaning on away! If he falls or has to catch himself, he was leaning. Do this every once in a while and ask your partner to do it for you. This will help you both stay on your own side.

When pushing, push your partner, but also compress into your forward leg as your "brake". The isometric structure of your legs will prevent you from overextending and leaning.

Remember to keep your shoulder blades connected down the back with the lats. Doing this and keeping the elbows sunk will help your arm weight go into your own body.

Even when pushing with a partner, a substantial piece of your attention should be on your own physical comfort and balance. When your partner entices you to overextend, use the sensing of your own body and your own comfort to feel your limit. Just because your partner invites you to overextend, lean and fall over does not mean you must do it! Just say "no" to leaning.

Chapter 5

Drills and Games Level 2

Listening to the Push:

Time frame: This drill will take only a moment to understand, but will remain useful for training flexibility and listening for many hours. As you progress, these skills will also be trained in more complex and interesting drills, so at some point you will probably leave this one behind.

Focus skills: Based on your ability to stick/adhere, we now work on the more advanced skills of listening (tien jing) and understanding (dong jing). This is a perceptual drill based on sensitivity in your skin at the point of contact with your partner, and with the ground. When receiving, practice feeling your partner's touch and your contact with the ground with great sensitivity. When pushing, feel from your feet, through your contact with your partner, for her center and connection with the earth. As your ability to listen develops you will become able to understand you partner's intent. On the surface this means being able to identify the precise vector of her force.

Photo 44

Format: Both stand in an enclosed stance. One person pushes slowly and persistently towards the other's center, modifying his push as his partner yields. Push slowly and gently to maximize your sensitivity. Start by pushing with one hand on your partner's crossed arms as in photo 44. In this and subsequent drills where you are pushing with one hand, some people put the free hand behind their waist or on the hip. This is formal and well disciplined. I prefer leaving it free to assist in balancing. When you are pushed, feel the push and yield to it with enough extension so that you can feel through the point of contact to your partner's feet. After you have pushed for a while switch roles.

Advanced variations: These variations are about changing the point of contact. First switch to pushing on your partner's ward off – having the point of contact away from the body on a defending arm will make it a little more difficult to listen and understand for both people.

Once this is working pretty well, try it with two hands pushing on crossed arms. The two points of contact will allow the pusher to triangulate and makes his job easier and the receiver's more difficult.

Next, move to two hands pushing on the wrists or forearms of your partner's arms while he holds them in a partially extended reach towards you. You should be pushing on the outside of the arms. To switch roles, switch hand positions.

Study questions: Some extension and muscle tone is required to have enough structure to allow the whole body to be impacted by your partner's touch. Only in this way will you be able to accurately perceive and understand the push. However, too much tone creates noise in your own body and drowns out sensitive perception. As you progress you should need less and less tone. How much is necessary for you now?

Is there an emotional attitude that allows greater perception? I would encourage you to practice humble curiosity. Could you get better at that? What makes it challenging?

<u>Skills you must learn here in order to progress</u>: You must have a clear experience of these jings: stick/adhere, listening and understanding. This takes time and practice. You must be able to balance "whole body as one unit" with "song, relaxed/loose/sunk" in a way that maximizes the clarity of your perception.

Single Hand Circling:

<u>Time frame:</u> This is a very common foundation drill in Yang, Wu and Chen styles. It will take only minutes to understand, but will remain useful for years. Because it is such an important foundation, (and thus should become very well known to you), it is a great context in which to study finesse as you become more advanced. Many people do not use it this way and discard it too early.

Use the joint circling from above when appropriate.

There are <u>many</u> variations of this drill.

<u>Focus skills:</u> Stick/adhere (tsan nien), listening (ting), receiving (tsou) and neutralizing (hua). Maintaining good structure as you practice these jings.

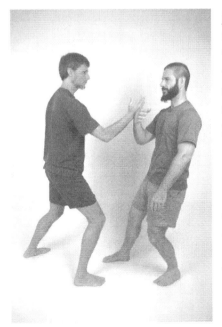

Photo 45

<u>Format:</u> Partners stand in an enclosed stance and touch the forward arms at the wrist (photo 45). Maintaining a light touch, draw a horizontal circle with the point of contact. If the right foot is forward, draw a counter-clockwise circle as seen from above. Keep shoulder down to elbow up to wrist and move at the leg joints more than at the arm joints. As your partner moves forward, you move back and vice versa.

Because of the direction of the circle (going across the forward leg), it is common for beginners to forget to keep the legs braced and the navel pointing the same direction as the weighted leg thus twisting their knees and ankles. Don't do that.

To start with, do this drill cooperatively, where the roles of yang (pusher) and yin (receiver) are not distinguished. If you have trained your sticking skills with earlier drills, this will be simple. Once you have the pattern, separate yin and yang so that there is a clear pusher and a clear receiver/follower.

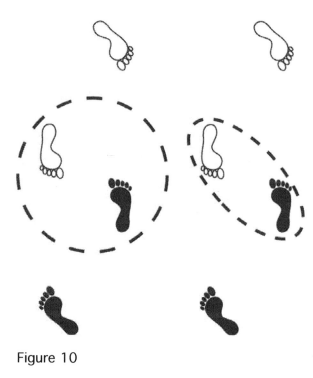

Once you make the shift to yin and yang, the shape drawn by the point of contact should change from a circle to an ellipse seen from above as shown in figure 10. A small ellipse is pictured, but it can move quite deeply into each person's stance. It is, unfortunately, common to see people push in a circle for some time without correction. This is due to an error in pushing. To describe a horizontal circle, the pusher has to push where his partner is not. Why would you do this?

The shape described by the point of contact is created by each person's push in turn. When it is your turn to push, push directly at your partner's center. For the most part, physical attacks are linear, like the flight of an arrow, as opposed to the game of seeking center where the push is like the flight of an attacking bee. In this drill, we mimic yielding to a punch, which is a linear attack.

Figure 10

The curves of the ellipse are created by the defender neutralizing and then pushing back. Practice making your neutralizing curve smaller and your push precisely targeted. This makes a slimmer ellipse. Make sure you do not use force when you neutralize.

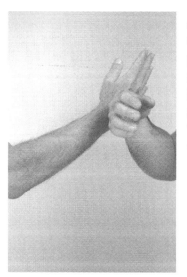

Advanced variations: As you get comfortable with this drill, allow the point of contact to roll at the wrist so that as you come forward your hand faces your partner in a "push" and as they push you, you roll into a "ward off". (Changing from photo 46 to 47).

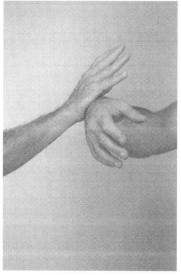

Photo 46

Photo 47

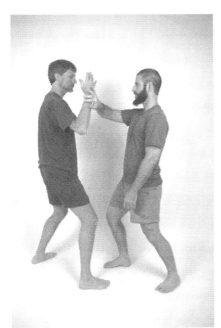

Photo 48

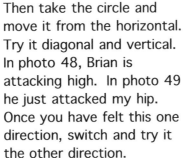Then take the circle and move it from the horizontal. Try it diagonal and vertical. In photo 48, Brian is attacking high. In photo 49 he just attacked my hip. Once you have felt this one direction, switch and try it the other direction.

Then go back into a horizontal ellipse, where the curves are small and the pushes are linear. When you are pushing, push towards where your see and feel your partner's center. When you are yielding, try to make your neutralizing curve smaller and the ellipse even more narrow.

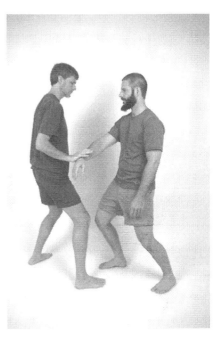

Photo 49

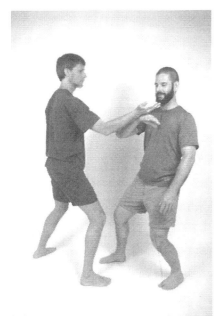

Photo 50

Try shifting back less and neutralizing faster. Make the ellipse shorter.

Experiment with pushing your partner at various different heights. If your partner reaches towards your head, you may well want to neutralize to an upward diagonal. If the push is low, you might neutralize by taking it lower. The level at which you deflect will impact the shape and position of your hand.

When your partner pushes low, try lowering your stance to store up more of her energy and then release it forward and up during your push.

Try this as a chopping motion to your partner's neck as in photo 50. With the right foot forward and using the right hand, the left side of the neck is threatened. With this, the neutralization may involve ducking. If you duck, do it more from the legs than just the neck.

In Chen style there is a variation of this called "Reeling and Rolling" which uses the wrists in specific ways. Here the shape described by the point of contact is essentially a diagonal line going from right side to right side (outside of the forward leg to the outside of the forward leg) when viewed from above (see figure 11).

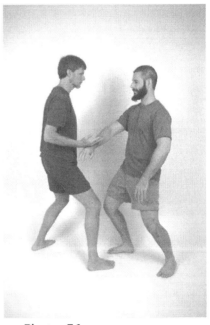

A pushes low and is deflected to B's right with his palm up, the back of his wrist covering the top of A's wrist. Then B pushes and A deflects in the same manner as shown in photo 51.

Also try one handed pushing in a mirror stance, where one partner has the right side forward and the other the left as in photo 52. Make contact with the forward hands at the wrists. As you reach towards your

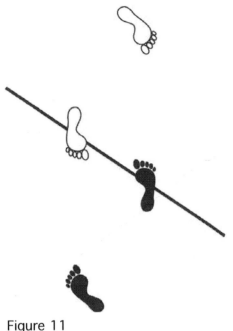

Figure 11

Photo 51

partner, she will roll the point to keep her hand between her body and your hand. Then she reaches towards you and you will circle your hand around hers. This changes the structure considerably and may feel awkward at first. The movement of the yang hand becomes more of a lunge. This drill is very similar to the kind of sticking drills that can be done with canes, staffs, spears, and swords.

<u>Study questions:</u> What are the useful and challenging aspects of circling on the horizontal, diagonal or vertical planes? Where do you run into tension or other challenges with your structure?

<u>Skills you must learn here in order to progress:</u> Your sticking and listening should be getting pretty developed. You must be able to circle from yin to yang on any plane and at different heights. You must be able to neutralize a push with the movement of your legs and waist. Your pushes should be targeted at your partner's center.

Photo 52

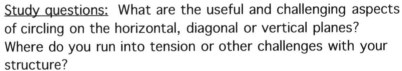

Closing the Forward Kua Exploration:

When you shift your weight forward, your stability is very different if your front kua is open or if it is closed. (If you do not yet specifically practice opening and closing your kua in your form, I recommend it.)

The one handed push drill is a great place to practice closing the front kua and to clearly experience the consequences. Try the following exploration in the pattern just described above.

- A pushes B with his right hand, both partner's right legs are forward.
- B sticks and yields to his left side. He has lots of room here and tries to entice A to come too far forward.
- A experiments with coming forward with an open kua as in photo 53 or settling into the hip and closing it as in photo 54.
- Once A stops coming in, B challenges A's balance by pulling at his wrist. Or, B changes to yang and pushes. The

Photo 53

Photo 54

question for you to study is; What are the changes of stability caused by the open or closed kua?

When you shift your weight forward, if you do not close the front kua, the tendency will be to push out of the rear foot and to slightly raise your center. If you are pushing and are enticed to do this, you will be in an unstable and vulnerable position to both a pull and a push.

However, if you close the kua, the tendency is to go <u>down</u>, dropping the rear knee slightly and sitting solidly in the front leg. If you are pulled in this posture, you should feel more solid, and if you are pushed you should feel more responsive.

Play with this and explore. Once you are really comfortable with it in the one handed push structure (and have found it in your form), integrate it into all your drills. Do not reach forward with your forward kua open!

Solo Pushing:

Time frame: This drill will take minutes to understand, but will remain useful for exploring and training your push for many hours.

Focus skills: Being able to push strongly with good structure (an jing).

To strengthen your push it is helpful to work with props.

If you have access to a heavy bag, you can play with pushing it. Experiment with pushing with one or two hands. When it comes back, connect with it and experiment with pushing it again. The first level of this is pushing the bag like a child on a swing. Then graduate to pushing the bag in more complex and disruptive patterns.

Try pushing long, short, with spin, and at different points in the bag's arc. As you explore these options make sure the push is coming from your legs and not just from your arms.

Photo 55

It can also be useful to push something really heavy. Cars are helpful for this. Vehicles that are shaped so you do not have to lean over to make contact are best. As you try these experiments, test the concerns I mentioned earlier about double weighting against your experience.

With the car in gear and the brake on so that it is not going to move, do a longer push from the rear as in photo 55. Use this as an opportunity to check your structure. Maintain the stress of the push. Try this with one and both hands with each leg forward. Experiment with how far your weight is forward before you start your push. At what point does your push feel strongest? You can do this with other immoveable objects, but cars are nice because you can get your forward foot beneath them.

Maintain good structure as you push – body upright, shoulder down to elbow up to wrist, elbow greater than 90'. Push on the exhale. Notice how you modify the position of the pelvis and lower back to be able to take the sustained pressure.

This clarifies the meaning of "body upright". Many people teach to do the form with the line of the spine being essentially "plumb erect" while maintaining the natural curves in the neck and lumbar. CMC was a proponent of this, while many traditional Yang stylists will incline the body forward (on a Brush Knee Twist for instance). When pushing or receiving a push, often keeping "plumb erect" is contra-indicated. When you push, allow your body to incline while maintaining a sense of length and extension in the spine. As you bend at the hip, the lumbar curve will also likely decrease ("sinking at the tail bone"). To get the right feel for this, make sure the muscular diaphragm of the pelvic floor (the perineum) is relaxed and spacious.

Next, with the car on a flat surface, in neutral and with the brake off, push the car forward with a longer push. Make sure it's not going to keep going into a lake! It might be necessary rock the car to get it to move. Stand in your forward stance with both hands on the car and push from your legs. Maintain good structure as you push – body upright, shoulder down to elbow up to wrist, elbow greater than 90'. Push on the exhale. Adjust your posture to take advantage of the movement of the car and keep pushing it.

Experiment also with doing short pushes against the side of a car (photo 56) to make use of its springs. Stand in a forward stance with your hands on the car, settle a bit into the rear leg to accumulate power, and then release it as a short, percussive push. Try this with one and both hands and with each leg forward. Maintain good structure as you push – body upright, shoulder down to elbow up to wrist, elbow greater than 90'. Push on the exhale. Rock the car, but do not dent it or hurt yourself!

Photo 56

Skills you must learn here in order to progress: You must be able to coordinate your movement so that single or double handed pushes are powered by your legs, directed by the waist and manifested through the arms and hands.

Pushing With a Partner:

Time frame: This drill will take a few minutes to understand, but will remain useful for training your targeting and pushing for many hours. Work with it for a few minutes each push hands session.

Focus skills: Being able to feel your partner enough to effectively target your push. This couples stick/adhere, listening and understanding with pushing. The receiver focuses on stick/adhere, listening, understanding, yielding and neutralizing. As the pusher, focus on stick/adhere, listening, understanding, and pushing through your partner's center towards his open door.

Format: Both standing in an enclosed stance, one person pushes with one or two hands on the other's crossed arms. Push slowly and gently through your partner's center. Use your touch to feel the center. With one hand, use your partner's attempts to twist you off to home in on his/her center. With two hands, add the vectors of your two pushes to triangulate through the center. This may mean that one hand traps or even entices forward and the other pushes.

After one person has pushed the other over several times, switch roles.

<u>Advanced variations:</u> Experiment with pushing up or down or to the sides. A classic strategy is to push downwards to break the root and then follow through upwards as your partner becomes light (which happens because he resists against the downward push). This can work even if done quite slowly.

Feel where your partner is substantial and insubstantial. The substantial line is usually through the center to the root. If you push directly on this line, you will get immovability until you overpower your partner's structure. This degrades into force against force very easily. Instead, when you find a substantial line, try using one hand to lightly maintain it and the other to push to your partner's open door.

Experiment with pushing slowly until your partner gives you some resistance, then stop the push for a moment. If he moves towards you, help him lightly to the side.

If you both agree to it, push more rapidly and more shallow. This is more percussive, like a strike, so be careful not to hurt your partner.

When you have your partner back and a bit pinned, experiment with imagining your energy pooling beneath him and floating him up. If you are receiving the push, drop your energy below this effort so that the push can not get beneath you. This can be a surprisingly effective method of attack and defense.

<u>Skills you must learn here in order to progress:</u> You must be able to accurately feel your partner's center, generate a push from your legs, and direct it through your target.

Uprooting:

<u>Time frame:</u> This drill will take awhile to understand because it has a lot of subtlety and parts to it. It will remain useful for training sensitive pushing and uprooting for many hours. Work with it for a few minutes each push hands session.

Uprooting is a flashy skill, fun to learn and use with your partner. It relies on understanding and borrowing your partner's force. It trains sensitivity and agile pushing. (For a formal description by physicist Robert Chuckrow, see his <u>The Tai Chi Book.)</u>

The next three photos (57, 58, 59) show me trapping and uprooting Brian. Very satisfying!

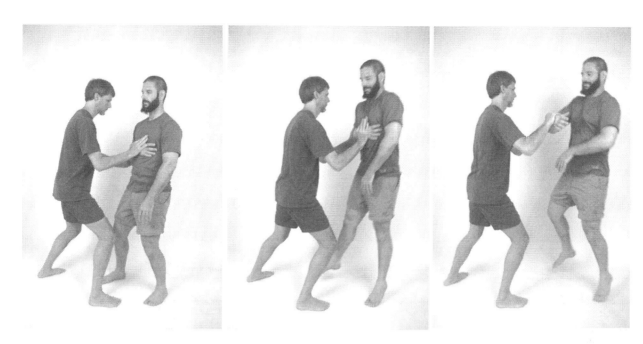

Photo 57   Photo 58   Photo 59

Since effective uprooting borrows your partner's force, let's talk about him first.

When you push your partner towards his rear open door, if he does nothing, he will fall over onto his back and hit his head. He is highly motivated not to allow this to happen. If he is actually falling, he will catch himself by moving his feet beneath him and moving his center away from you. If you push him while he is purposefully moving his center and feet away from you, you will support his motion and increase the speed with which he moves away from you.

As you push him horizontally with two hands back towards his open door he will either fall through it, or struggle. If he struggles and stiffens against you, release him for a brief moment. Without you to push against, he starts to fall forward and then catches himself. Just support his catch (which is a push of his own towards the rear) and borrow that force to push him back even farther.

If you push him horizontally, he will feel light and step back easily. If you push him on a downward diagonal, he will first have to overcome the downward force in order to move his feet. He does this by pushing against the ground with his legs to brace against your downward pressure. Once he is pushing against the ground, if you release your downward pressure and push only horizontally, he will fly up with his force and horizontally with yours. This can look very impressive.
Try these with a cooperative partner. Keep it slow and feel the dynamics I have described above.

Once you've got that, make it more intense for him by pushing back and a little down. As you push him back and down towards his open door, he is even more likely to struggle. Now he is bracing both forward and up, and when you release him, his center rises along with his fall forward. When you support his catching himself now, you can threaten to push him downwards again. Out of fear of falling and hitting his head, he will push against the floor to free his feet. No problem! Now push him back and up to support the direction he is already moving. "Houston, we have a lift off! "

Work with this uprooting pattern to make these skills more and more automatic. Try to do a little of this drill every time you push with a partner. Many teachers have special walls set up to push students into. Some maintain that the percussive strike of hitting the wall strengthens the body over time.

Traditionally, it is a demonstration of good form and control, when uprooted, to hop back on one leg until the momentum is spent. This is a good practice because if you are hopping on one foot you are not tripping over yourself and stumbling backwards. Stumbling is not only undignified, but may also make you fall on your butt (even more undignified).

CMC would combine his uprooting with stepping in with his forward foot and allowing his rear foot to follow at the conclusion of the push. In this way, he effectively put his center where his partner's used to be. His partner, invariably, went flying. I describe the details of this stepping pattern later in this workbook.

Correcting Your Partner's Errors in Pushing:

Time frame: This drill will take a few minutes to understand and only a couple hours of practice to make smooth. Once you have it, it can be integrated smoothly into later drills.

Focus skills: As the receiver, stick/adhere, listening, understanding, and yielding with a focus on neutralizing. As the pusher, stick/adhere, listening, understanding, with a focus on pushing through the center. This drill applies an elbow circle freeing a backfist to the face.

Format: Both people stand in an enclosed stance as if doing the one handed push drill. Do one handed pushing for a while with a linear push. As you receive the push, be attentive to your partner's targeting errors. If the push is smoothly on your center it will be difficult to neutralize. However, when it is off to one side, a hole develops in your partner's forward intent through which you can neutralize and strike. To learn this drill, your partner has to push a bit off center on purpose.

- Brian (B) is in a right foot forward, right ward off. I (A) push with my right hand on B's right wrist, missing his center by pushing too far to B's left. As A comes in, B turns to his left with the push. His right elbow points towards B. (A may recognize this elbow as a threat and might want to bring his left hand up to protect himself.)

- A continues to push off center to B's left and B uses the pressure to compress his body like a series of springs. B slips his left hand under A's right wrist (photo 60).

- At the proper time, B uses his left hand to brush B's right push off (photo 61) allowing his right hand to spring forward in a back fist to the A's face. Don't hit B!

- B can use his left hand to catch or deflect the backfist (photo 61).

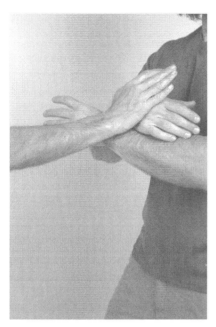

I liken this exercise to those elastic band shooting guns where the elastic is stretched and when the trigger is pulled the elastic is released to fly. Here your body and back fist are the elastic, and when your left hand slips the blockage of the incoming push off, they fly forward without hesitation.

Most people have difficulty with the "without hesitation" part, so expect that and work to eliminate this problem.

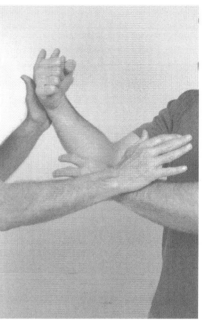

Photo 60

Photo 61

Next make the push too far to the other side as Brian is doing, pushing off center to my right in photo 62.. As the push comes in, close the forward kua to roll it off and attack with the rear hand (photo 62). These kinds of responses effectively motivate your partner to focus his push!

Once you have both received with each foot and arm forward and you feel comfortable with the mechanics of striking when the push is off center, do the one handed circling drill and move to strike your partner whenever his/her push is off your center. This will gradually train each of you to push effectively on the center. Who wants to be hit, after all?

A caution: This is a drill that may be viewed as impolite by folks who have not trained it. I have often begun a friendly session of one handed push hands with a new partner only to find that s/he is not pushing me on my center. Most people respond better to a verbal comment on this than a backfist to the face!

Photo 62

Skills you must learn here in order to progress: You need to know how to feel and push directly on your partner's center. You need to be able to neutralize these off center pushes easily in a way that let's your partner know she was pushing off center.

Snake Arms:

Often you will push with a person who does not have the skills to force you to keep your arms in defensive ward off structures. In these cases, you may be able to stick/adhere, listen, understand, yield and neutralize while allowing your arms to move like snakes. This is a good skill to have (hence the drill) but it only works with pushes that do not effectively threaten your center. More focused pushes must be dealt with by moving the whole body as one unit and maintaining a good defensive ward off structure.

Photo 63

Time frame: This drill will take a few minutes to understand and only a couple hours of practice to make smooth. Once you have it, it can be integrated smoothly into later drills. It is a more advanced version of Sticking with wrists from level one.

Format: Both people stand in an enclosed stance touching at both wrists (photo 63). The person pushing moves in, pushing at the wrists, the person being pushed moves each arm to stick/adhere, listen, understand, yield and neutralize. This will entail less retreating with the body and more snaking the arms around. Despite that, keep your arms connected to your center with enough muscle tone and extension. Move your arms from your legs and waist and yield in order to neutralize. When you have neutralized, switch to pushing and allow your partner to snake. See if you can neutralize with one arm even as you snake and spiral the other one forward.

As you are yielding, try to find ways for the snaking arms to move into pushing. In order to do this drill. When you push, keep the focus of the vectors of your push somewhat diffuse. This will allow your partner the leeway to snake.

Advanced variations:
Try spiraling your snake arms up your partner's arms. See if you can trap him by pushing back on his elbows and binding his shoulders (photo 64).

Photo 64

68

Try pinning his elbows to his sides (photo 65).

As the trapped partner, rest for a moment and really let yourself feel trapped. Then shift your body back while your arms stay in place (photo 66) this will give you the space to counter (photo 67). Or you might turn the waist and free one arm first (photo 68). These are actually fairly easy traps to free yourself from by yielding and sinking.

Photo 65

Photo 66

Photo 67

Photo 68

Study questions: Once you can spiral your arms easily up to your partner's elbows, see if you can spiral up to his shoulders to push there. What kind of traps happen at the shoulders? How can you adapt the freeing strategies of yielding and sinking here? (Hint: refer back to the shoulder variation of the weight shifting drill from Chapter 3.)

Once you are both comfortable with snaking the arms, focus the vectors of your push through your partner's center to his open door. If you end up in a position where your arms are trapped or pinned, and your body doesn't understand how to get out of it yet, set that same trap up again on purpose. Feel and explore the bind. Then sink and move the body back away from your arms just enough so that you can find peng and freedom. Turn your waist to make it easier.

When you receive a push, snake when you can. Snaking tells your partner that his push is too diffuse. If your partner is able to snake on you focus your push more precisely.

Skills you must learn here in order to progress: You must have a focused push that threatens your partner's center and a working feeling for vectors. You must be able to do snakey, spiraling motions with your arms that allow you to neutralize in the arms.

Often there are moments, even with skilled partners, where they are not able to push you clearly through your arms to your center. In this case, even if there is not enough space to allow your whole body to slip towards his/her center, often there will be enough for your arms or hands. You must be able to use snaking, spiraling arm techniques to slip through and create more room for your returning push. This situation is also a great place to use press (jhee) in its meaning as "squeeze through or into".

Free Form Game 2: Fixed Step Freestyle Push Hands

You now have the skills to make the game of push hands even more interesting. Your goal is to knock your partner off balance while she tries to do the same to you. Avoid using the strength of the upper body – push from your legs. The person who moves a foot first is defined as the loser. Of course it is better to move a foot than to fall.

No grabbing, kicking or striking is allowed though pushing and pulling is. Show respect for your partner by not attacking the groin, breasts, neck, eyes or head. In this game, push as if trying to keep a beach ball underwater - as you push the ball down it will roll and spin to come up - to keep it under you will need to compensate. Similarly, as your partner shifts and turns to yield to and try to neutralize your push, readjust to continue pushing through her center. The push is no longer like an arrow, unable to re-aquire the target when it moves. Now your push is like a fox chasing a rabbit, changing instantly to respond to your partners evasions.

Grabbing on to your partner to prevent falling (as I am doing in photo 69) is bad form and is an invitation for your partner to crash (shoulder stroke) into you. The same is true if you pull your partner in to your center (photo 70). However, do hold on to your partner when necessary to keep either of you safe. Often you will see teachers pushing a student over and catching her at the wrist with the other hand to make sure she does not get hurt.

Photo 69

Stay in verbal contact as you are playing and make the game

Photo 70

as fun as possible for both of you. Laugh when you are knocked over and compliment your partner when she gets you with a good push (builds humility)!

Format: Both stand in an enclosed stance. One person pushes slowly and persistently towards the other's center, modifying his push as his partner yields. Push with both hands on whatever your partner gives you to push on. If you can, slip from pushing on his arms to pushing on his body. Photos 71 and 72 show some of the situations that may arise in this game.

Go back and forth, maintaining good leg, hip structure and body upright. This game is best done quite slowly with sensitivity, but also try it faster for more dynamic fun.

Photo 71

Photo 72

When you push, always push towards an open door. When receiving, always receive into a leg.

Photo 73

Photo 74

Advanced variations:

This pattern can also be done facing each other with each person's feet parallel (photos 73,74). The width of your stance can vary from a wide horse (riding) stance to a narrow goat (riding) stance. Stand close enough so that you can rest your palms on your partner's shoulders. Once again, push on whatever your partner gives you to push on.

Start by simply pushing each other slowly straight on to refine your structure and find your root/structure (and its limits). Each of you is in a precarious stance.

Once you have that, add in neutralizing, turning the waist, and bending the knees more. When you are pushed back, twist in the waist looking right or left. Turning to the right extends your left arm toward your partner and vice versa. Bending forward and arching back can extend your possibilities here. Remember to counter-balance. Raising one hand to attack while lowering the other to pull is another version of counter-balancing.

Once you are comfortable with this done slowly, speed it up to play more freely. Take turns having one person attack and the other defend.

Another variation: Push hands usually starts with the hands connected. What happens if you start with the hands not yet connected? A real attacker, of course, will start that way after all! To develop comfort with this, try this is an enclosed stance. Define who is attacking and start slowly. When you are defending, reach your hands towards your partner to connect with any strike early. Recognize that we are not yet allowing movement of the feet, which limits the attacker's momentum, but it is still hard to defend against a full speed punch to the nose without moving the feet. If you like playing in a more martial way I highly recommend exploring some Chi Sau (sticky hands) and other drills from Wing Chun.

Try to integrate all the skills you have been practicing into whatever version of this game you are playing. Check that your posture is good and that your eyes are in soft focus so that you can see your partner's entire body while letting your gaze rest on the hollow of his throat. Seek advantageous opportunities:

- to root
- to neutralize while still forward or only once you have gotten your partner to almost expend her push
- to uproot
- to correct her errors by striking (feints only!)
- to snake if her push is diffuse
- to focus on the process of learning more than the goal of winning
- to focus on the goal of winning more than the process of learning (just for fun!)

At this point you have enough skills to make the game very interesting and to be able to start pushing with people from other schools or styles. Doing some of this might be fun for you. This is good experience for you but do not lose sight of the careful non-competitive training that is required to master T'ai Chi tui shou skills. Be warned that if you teach this game to a person who has not trained in this as you have, his attention is likely going be on the competitive goal of pushing you over. He will use strength and guile to overpower you, and even couch potatoes may be successful. Yet another opportunity to practice humility!

These matches can be very instructive. Do not be discouraged if you get knocked over a lot. As much as you are able, stick to your skills and do not get seduced into using force against force in order to save face, or out of frustration. Patient training of sticking, adhering, joining and following will lead to unusual skills and eventually you will be pushed over only rarely.

We have more points to remember when moving with a partner now:

- Maintain your own structure first! Preserve the ability to spin on your center line by keeping your vertical extension and alignment as you shift your weight back and forth.

- Let your eyes rest on the hollow of your partner's neck. In this way you will not be distracted by her eyes, while being able to see her gaze and her whole body with your peripheral vision.

- Stick to your partner, do not avoid or separate from her. Do not lean. Direct your attention through the point of contact to your partner's center.

- Wait for her to initiate and follow her movement.

- Do not oppose or resist her movement, but by joining and following gain a superior position (arrive first).

- Push at the edges of your partner's solidity, like stream water flowing around a rock.

- In being pushed, receive it first. Extend from the earth, through your center to the point of contact. Then yield first with the legs, then with the arms and lastly with the body.

- Pull, but do not grab (to preserve your balance).

73

- Pay attention to yours and your partner's closed and open doors.

- Combine vectors to push – use both a strong and a tuning hand.

- Avoid force against force.

- Make use of opening and closing your kua.

Chapter 6

Higher Level Internal Skills

Yi, or Attention/Intent:

Ultimately in solo and partner practice, we want our chi and movement to be guided by our intent. In learning new skills, we go through 4 stages:
- Unconscious incompetence – we don't know we can't do it.
- Conscious incompetence- we know we can't do it.
- Conscious competence – we can only do it if we pay active attention.
- Unconscious competence – we do it without thought.

We can look at these stages in learning to drive a car. We go from the unconscious incompetence of infancy to the conscious incompetence of the child. Then when we start learning, there is a lot to keep track of and we can only drive effectively if we think about it. Coming up to a turn in my parent's old VW, I thought, "Ok, turn signal, brake, clutch, downshift, turn." Fortunately, all this becomes automatic after a while, freeing more attention up to talk on cell phones, listen to the radio, and snack!

Today, when I get in the car, I drive with my intent to get from point A to point B (product) safely and legally (process).

Similarly, when we first learn the T'ai Chi form, there is a great deal of self–monitoring to do it correctly. As we improve, attention is freed up for finer and finer details. As we improve further, we can rest more in our intent to stay in sensitive and responsive alignment (process) while executing the specific application (product).

Part of the intent is the goal and part is the feeling in the body as we achieve the goal (process). So our intent includes both product and process (For you bodyworkers, recall Alexander's concerns with end-gaining in the Alexander Technique).

As you develop greater skill in push hands, make sure that you continue to refine your intent. The process portion remains the same; keeping the body safe, in sensitive and responsive alignment and following the principles. The goal is to gain the advantage over your partner.

As an example, I have pushed with people who would slavishly push my arm even when they had an opportunity to slip from my arm and push my body. This is ok during a drill, but a manifestation of unclear intent during a game. Gain control of your partner's center by maintaining your intent to do so. If your partner is neglectful enough to give you access to his torso, let him know by taking advantage of it.

One of the challenges of training is making the process realistic while limiting the danger. Intent is a crucial part of this. When I train, my intent is to gain the clear upper hand while staying safe and following the T'ai Chi principles. Physically violating the principles in order to knock my partner over doesn't cut it. Going past gaining the upper hand to humiliating or unintentionally injuring my partner (out of anger, pride or insensitivity) is also a violation of principles.

Personally, I see refining my intent as a study of my relationship with the Tao. Opportunities to practice abound – for instance, how can I notice but allow my breath? How can I stand in wu chi and allow my body to move naturally? How can I take this to the form? How can I maintain self-discipline without being harsh with myself? How can I do the same with my children? How can I defend myself freely without going overboard?

When a person attacks me, superficially, he wants to hurt me. This is an expression of his pain, but is also an attempt to get his deeper needs met. I prefer not to have people try to meet their needs by hurting me! But at the same time I can recognize as human and legitimate the desire to get those needs met. Fundamentally, I work the same way (even if the methods I use to get my needs met are different).

The struggle that is real for me today is: How can I stand up for and honor my preferences (to stay safe) while at the same time remaining interested in you getting your needs met as well? Is there some way that I can stay safe and at the same time help my attacker get what he wants deep inside? Remember, the highest level of self-defense is preventing violence and preserving life. There is nothing in there about denying the existence of conflict and disagreements.

These musings are of importance to me because the intent that I really want, the intent that will free my power up the most, is the one that allows me to fully express myself without violating you or trying to eliminate your right to try to get your needs met. How do I apply this to a physical or emotional violation of my space? These concerns may seem a little philosophical, but I assure you that fully freeing up your natural power requires dealing with them.

Do you have some of these concerns as well? What are some of the core intentions that you hold? How do you balance your needs and preferences with those of others?

Mental Toughness

In modern sports and coaching, we recognize that players perform best when they are in the proper frame of mind. Many athletes talk about being in the "zone", where they are at their best and feel unbeatable. If being in the zone is a ten, feeling discouraged, tight and self-critical is more like a one. You could evaluate your own state right now - or at any other time - on this continuum. Your ability to achieve peak performance varies, and there are characteristic features of your peak performance state. Mental toughness is the ability to recognize and maintain your peak performance state under pressure.

The pressure that we experience in push hands occurs on several levels. The first is the obvious physical challenge. Then there is the emotional challenge to remain calm while having your balance tested. And lastly there is the internal challenge to our relationship with ourselves when we have experiences we don't want (like being knocked over). Mental toughness deals with these last two challenges.

As you interact with a variety of push hands partners, you will be physically challenged or pushed over again and again. If you are actively using this workbook, you should be getting plenty of opportunity to experience and study the physical and emotional tension that occurs immediately prior to be knocked over!

Let's take a few pages to examine this experience and see how we might work with it. In doing so, I'll relate this to how these challenges occur in everyday relationships as well.

When your partner pushes you effectively in a direction that is not comfortable, your habitual reaction is likely to become anxious, defensive and physically more tight.

When my children behave in a way that is not comfortable for me, I have the very same habitual reaction. In fact, whenever I:
1) have an experience I do not want or
2) do not have the experience I do want
I have this same kind of habitual reaction. Most people do not notice that there is an opportunity for choice here, but instead go into their unique habitual response marked by physical tension and some kind of self-protective behavior.

For most of us, this occurs dozens of times a day in small and large situations. Most people go with the habit and become anxious, defensive and physically more tight. Often they will also bolster their position with self-righteousness (which is the process of telling themselves that it is right and appropriate to have their habitual response).

Let's consider this in an example of road rage. On the way to his T'ai Chi class, Harry is cut off on the freeway. Feeling angry, he tells himself that the other driver should not have done that and is wrong and bad. He feels superior to the other driver and unfairly wronged. He feels angry and physically tight in his neck and shoulders.

What do you think, does this do Harry any good? Does it make him a more skillful driver? Does it help him feel centered and at peace? Does it move him towards the experience that he wants? Personally, I answer "No." to all these questions.

Despite being cut off, Harry makes it on time to class. Through doing the warm ups and the form he regains his sense of peace. But in the push hands practice, Suzanne challenges his balance several times. Not enjoying feeling his vulnerability, he becomes self-critical. He determines to not allow her to do that again. He becomes tight and defensive and does not allow her to express her push enough for him to effectively neutralize it. Instead he relies on force against force, is able to overpower Suzanne, and tells himself that now he is doing better.

At the same time, Suzanne was feeling pretty good about knocking Harry over and is not totally sure why the results of her efforts have changed. What she does know is that now she is being knocked over and that Harry's push feels harsh. A part of her falls into self-criticism while another part is trying to figure out how Harry is wrong for pushing her in a way that feels uncomfortable to her.

Again, we can ask about Harry and Suzanne: do their emotional and cognitive reactions do either of them any good? Do they improve their push hands skills? Do they help them feel centered and at peace? Do they move them towards the experience that they want? That would be a "No." from me again.

Harry and Suzanne are both knocked off center because neither has enough mental toughness.

Mental toughness is an inside job.
The first step is to articulate for yourself the experiential features of your peak state – a ten. When you are there:
- What physical sensations are you having?
- How is your breathing?
- What are you saying to yourself?
- In what tone of voice?
- What images are you playing yourself?
- What are your beliefs about yourself, what you can expect from others and the universe in general?
- How do you feel about yourself, others and the universe in general?

It can be useful to contrast this with the experiential features of a one – an ineffective state – by asking the same questions so that you can starkly compare these states.

In general, peak performance states are marked by:
- Relaxed, flowing sensations
- Full and regular breathing coordinated with any movement
- Encouraging self talk in a respectful and kind tone
- Encouraging and centering images
- Positive beliefs about yourself, others and the universe in general
- Good feelings about yourself, others and the universe

Let's imagine that Harry has an epiphany, understands this and really commits to maintaining his peak effective state. Now he can invest in loss with this! Every challenge to his state reveals the places of strength and weakness in his stance. When he gets knocked off by the behavior of a fellow driver, a family member or his push hands partner, he notices that he has been knocked off and does what is necessary to regain his emotional center. Sometimes he even perceives the opportunity to go into his tight, anxious and defensive habit and passes it up! This is real and valuable personal growth.

Physically in push hands, I expect to find myself in uncomfortable positions and to need to purposefully move to improve my comfort again and again. Emotionally, I expect the same thing, that I will get scared, defensive, self righteous, pissed off, self-critical (you name it!) and that I will have to re-center emotionally again and again.

Eventually, we get good at re-centering and it becomes rapid and habitual, but at first it will be slow and frustrating.

Physically we can re-center by locating our center-line and tantien and responsively maintaining the integrity of our posture despite changing outer conditions. On an emotional level, we can identify our peak performance state and responsively maintain that in the face of constantly changing outer conditions.

I know that I am unable to perfectly maintain either my center-line or my peak state, so I practice noticing when I am off and re-centering on purpose.

In the beginning of self-defense practice, we defend a large space and feel self-righteously angry when this space is violated. This leads to tension, emotional upset and the desire for retaliation. At this stage we are like a defensive teen or a belligerent drunk.

As we practice, we identify our center and the space we choose to defend becomes smaller. We begin to recognize that responding with tension, anger and self-righteous retaliation to slights and insults is costly and does not lead us towards our center or peace. The old habits, however, are hard to interrupt and we have to work hard first to notice them in action and then replace them. Success comes slowly, but gradually as we practice our sense of personal peace in the face of changing conditions increases.

Our target is to have complete faith in both our perception of our center in relation to external conditions and to our wisdom and skill in responding to the changes in a way that leads us back towards comfort and peace.

The well-known author and lecturer Wayne Dyer points out that when you squeeze an orange, what comes out is what is inside – orange juice. What comes out when life puts the squeeze on you? What do you want to come out? Push hands drills are designed to train you to relax under pressure and to be able to maintain your peace of mind despite physical and emotional insults.

Cultivating   Compassion

An important aspect of my personal high performance state and peace of mind is the combination of loving kindness and clear perception that is compassion. As I struggle with remaining calm under pressure, I direct this compassion towards myself. As I push my partner, I feel compassion for his struggle. My target here is to be able to feel compassion for myself and the other in the heat of conflict.

I know that my habit is to retaliate self-righteously to hurts, insults and attacks. And I also know that doing so is not the level of skill to which I aspire. The tension and outrage that arise in me when I feel wronged interfere with my skill. This is the deep challenge of push hands and the T'ai Chi approach to conflict. I know that my habitual response is outdated and that it comes from efforts of my cerebral cortex to categorize the world. But "the Tao that can be spoken is not the eternal Tao". The response I cultivate is one that relies on deeper brain structures, before the separation of right and wrong (yin and yang, me and you). As Rumi says, "There is a field out beyond right and wrong. I'll meet you there." In this realm, energy, motion and momentum impacts my body and I respond to them in a way that leads me to greater comfort and peace.

Physically I do this by attending to my center line and tan tien and moving to regain comfort. I preserve and regain my emotional center by practicing compassion and not taking the action of others or "acts of God" personally (agreement #2 of Ruiz's Four Agreements).

Sneaky Energy Manipulations

It can be fun to use sneaky energy manipulations on your partner from time to time. A simple one is to run his energy backwards on his Conception Vessel.

The Conception Vessel is a meridian that runs up the midline of the front of the torso. Vividly imagining and intending your partner's energy to run down the midline of the front of his body will weaken him for a short time. Try it. Give your partner an ordinary push to get a "before" picture. Then just before you push him the next time, run his energy down his midline. Push him again. A little play with this and you will be able to produce very clear results.

Some people will say that this is not "sporting", and I would agree with them. So experiment openly with this with your training partners. And don't hesitate to use this with people who are threatening you – draining an attacker's energy is a completely legitimate way to reduce violence.

Another sneaky manipulation is to feel and imagine pooling your energy beneath your partner's feet as you push. Literally imagine your energy cutting him off from the earth. This will make him lighter and more easily knocked over.

These and other manipulations can be used to give you an advantage. They also point out that for your own protection it's important to keep your positive, energy enhancing visualizations strong. There are many kinds of "psychic protection" imagery that can be helpful here. One version that works well for fixed step drills is to imagine your whole body sheathed in a protective layer of light. The light is nourished through your feet, so they are firmly rooted through the bubbling well (Kidney 1) with tendrils of energy connecting to the Earth's core. The light glows with the fullness of the breath, so your breath is deep, full and thin. Get this visualization strong and see what happens when your partner then tries to drain your energy or pool beneath you.

Chapter 7

Drills and Games Level 3

Fixed Step Two Handed Patterns:

As you and your partners become more skillful, it is time to work on the formal structures of two handed push hands. Here are several. These begin as drills to get the pattern, but then should become less formal games. You will need to drill each pattern for awhile (hours) in order to understand the framework and the variations and change overs from side to side and hand to hand.

These games sometimes have only subtle differences in terms of timing and application. So expect to find learning them somewhat challenging and do not be surprised if you switch from one to the other without meaning to. The point of these games is to train your arms to be able to control and defend the space in front of you (and ultimately, to no longer rely on the arms). Switching spontaneously to another pattern may be a manifestation of skill or it may be due to a lack of understanding. Be honest with yourself and drill conscientiously.

I recommend that you continue to mix drills and games in your practice sessions, so add these patterns in slowly to your repertoire. Because these are more complex, give yourself plenty of time to make sense of the instructions and pictures.

In use, often partners will start by following a formal structure for a few cycles and then go to free form at will. Returning to the formal structure from time to time within the flow can be a good way to re-center and ensure that your defense is strong.

If you push with a variety of people, you will find that very few people know all these forms and that this limits their understanding of what is possible. Each of these forms can continue to teach you subtleties for many years.

Simple two handed push hands:

Time frame: This pattern will take three minutes to understand and only a couple hours of practice to make smooth. Once you have it, it can be integrated into later drills.

Format:
- Start in an enclosed stance with one person in a two handed push (A) at the other's right wrist and elbow.
- The person yielding (B) is in a right ward off, his left reaching to the side of A's right arm (photo 75).

Photo 75

- B shifts back with A's push and turns towards his right elbow. As the neutralization is complete, B brings his left hand to push at A's right elbow while rolling his right wrist to push at A's wrist.

- Now B pushes and A yields towards his right elbow. Photo 76 shows me (A) having turned to my right in response to Brian's (B's) push.
- Photo 77 shows me having settled to push on Brian's right arm. As I come forward, he will lift his left to touch my right elbow.
- Each person is being pushed on the same arm (right) as you cycle back and forth.

This has four versions, one each with a right or left arm ward off with the right leg forward and then the left leg forward. Try each one. Be sure to maintain good physical structure and alignment.

Photo 76

Photo 77

Details:

The hand at the wrist pushes more on the forearm than the palm. If you push on the back of the palm, your partner has another degree of freedom due to the free wrist joint. If you are on the forearm and do not contact the wrist you miss the information from that joint. If you push with your fingers the pressure can hyper-extend your fingers. If you push with the wrist itself, you lose dexterity. These limits define the placement of the hand on the wrist. About 2/3 of the hand is on the forearm with the heel of the hand in contact with the bottom of your partner's arm.

The hand at the elbow can make use of the sensitivity of the fingers. The hollow of the hand is on the bone of the forearm at the elbow (ulna). The angle of the hand may be more vertical when pushing, or may turn to horizontal to give the fingers access to the upper arm to control the joint more effectively. This hand is often the tuning hand in the push and thus the contact should be light and precise.

In many push hands patterns you will push consistently on one arm. This leads to needing to "change over" to push on the other arm after a time. Once you fully understand the particular drill or game, train the change over so that it is as fluid and comfortable as the rest of the pattern. Often there are dynamic reasons that might lead you to do the change over and advantages that develop for the person who initiates the change.

Here's the change over for this pattern:

When you are fully pushed back, absorbing your partner's energy and have almost fully neutralized, it is possible to change which of your partner's arms you push back on. To do so from the right sided push as described above, replace your right elbow with your left hand and move your right hand to his left elbow. You can do the replacement by bringing your left arm under (photos 78, 79) or over (photos 80, 81) your partner's pushing arms.

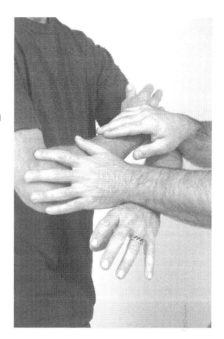

Photo 78

When you do the replacement, make it subtle, without jarring

Photo 79

or scraping your partner's arms. Ideally, in the dark, one should be able to replace without the other person knowing. Do this by taking the pressure of your partner's left hand push onto a new point of contact on your left hand, brushing up (if under) or down (if over) while at the same time melting away with your right elbow. Then place your right hand on his left elbow and push.

This pattern has eight versions, one each for going over or under with a right or left arm ward off with the right leg forward and then the left leg forward. Each one has a slightly different feel and structure. Try each one. If you have yielded effectively, there should be no sense of having to rush this transition. Be sure to maintain good physical structure and alignment.

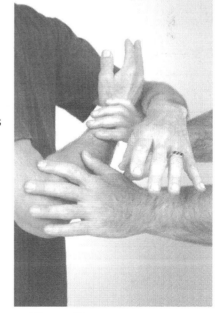

Photo 80

Photo 81

A common error here is to try to do the change over with the wrong timing. Make the change as you switch from yin to yang, immediately upon neutralizing.

Generally the person who does the change over has a momentary advantage because it breaks the rhythm of the movement. An effective way to practice this is to have one person do the change overs at a time. Practice doing each of the four change overs with one leg forward, then switch roles. Then switch feet and each do the four with this foot forward. Once you and your partner are comfortable with these change overs, integrate them into the game and make use of them in a way that is responsive to the flow of the moment.

Another point to notice in this and the other games is that when you are doing a yang push on a forearm, the hand that is on your partner's elbow can tilt that elbow up. If your partner is stiff, this lever can disrupt his center. If your partner is not stiff, both your hands are attached to one of his and this leaves his other hand available for mischief!

Once you have drilled these movements so they are comfortable and you are freely playing this as a game, go back and check your postures and reduce the amount of tension in the movements. Recall the fundamental rules of push hands:
- Stick to your partner, do not avoid or separate from her.
- Wait for her to initiate and follow her movement.
- Do not oppose or resist her movement, but by joining and following gain a superior position (arrive first).

Check on the application of your vectors to insure that you are not using force against force and check that you are not doing any of the three types of double-weighting or leaning.

This self check process is important to do as you work with each of the next patterns also. These are more difficult and challenging to learn from a book, but if you have built your foundation by doing the preceding drills and games, you will be able to get them.

Martial Application   Variation:

One variation of this pattern focuses on changing from rollback to pluck and split in order to attack your partner's arm.

- Starting from the above example, as A pushes on B's right arm, B rolls back to his right towards the elbow of the ward off.
- B's right hand rolls the point to grasp A's right wrist and pulls it back and down to his right. Meanwhile he pushes against the back of A's right elbow with his left hand (photo 82) seeking to hyper-extend A's arm at the elbow (gently in the drill).
- A allows his body and arm to go with B's pull and then sinks his elbow and twists his arm CW. This twist allows him to protect his elbow and roll the point and prepares to grasp B's right wrist in turn (photo 83).
- Now A pulls B's right arm and threatens B's elbow with his left forearm. Notice that Brian is preferring to attack with his hand in photo 82 while I am attacking with my forearm in photo 84. Use whatever weapon is most comfortable for you.

Go back and forth, coordinating your weight shift with your arm movements to create power.

Photo 83

Photo 82   Photo 84

This drill, because it is about grabbing and twisting each other's arms, easily degenerates into force against force. Be mindful of that and do your best to stay soft. When the yang movement requires structure, precision and power it is naturally difficult to then switch to the yin jings of yielding, sticking and following.

Practice all four hand and foot combinations of this variation.

Cheng Man-Ch'ing's (CMC'S) Push Hands:

<u>Time frame:</u> This will take ten minutes to understand and a few hours of practice to make smooth. This pattern is based on simple two handed push hands with a change over each time. It is one of my favorites and has given me many hours of challenge and delight.

Photo 85

<u>Format:</u>
- Both stand in an enclosed stance with A in a two handed push at B's right wrist and elbow. B is in a right ward off with his left arm reaching forward to touch A's right elbow with his left fingers (photo 85).

- B yields and turns towards his right elbow. The arms are carried, moving because the torso moves. Initiate the movement from the legs, pelvis and waist. B's left hand, in contact with A's right elbow, helps deflect A to B's right. B sinks his left elbow with his lat to keep the arm attached to the turn of his torso (photo 86).

Photo 86

Photo 87

- As the push is neutralized to the side, A rolls the point at his right wrist, moves the left hand and executes press on his right wrist (photo 87). A's press allows him to re-center his attack. B maintains his right ward off and does not allow his right arm to be compressed against his body – instead he yields with his whole body to his left.

- B moves his left hand to "sandwich" A's hands with his and rolls back to his left side. He turns through the waist in response to A's press (photo 88). See photo 89 for a close up of the "hand sandwich".

Photo 88

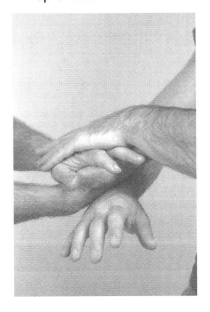

Photo 89

- B rolls the point with his left hand ending up in push at A's left wrist, and moves his right to push on A's left elbow (photo 90). A's right arm will soon extend to connect at the forearm with B's elbow. Now B gets to push and press, while A yields first to his left then to the right.

At first, do this pattern as a drill, collaborating to get a nice flow going. To do this, both people use their sensitive sticking energy at all times and neither should be challenging the other's balance. Once you have a sense of the flow, then start to separate yin and yang (yielding and attacking).

This pattern has a clear ward off, roll back, push and press. Use this to make your expression of these energies clear and distinct from one another.

Photo 90

Once you have the flow, it is essential with more complicated push hands forms to clearly distinguish between yin and yang in terms of your intent. At each moment, be either attacking or defending. Allow your mental/emotional attitude to change with your intent. This form has two attacks and two defensive movements. Your job when doing the (yang) push and press is to locate your partner's center and push or press through it.

Your job when doing the (yin) rollbacks is to stick to your partner and join with and follow his movement while seeking the opportunity to neutralize.

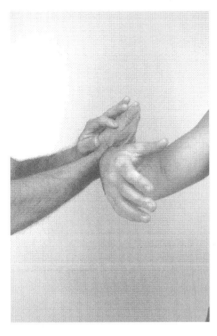

This is the first pattern where we are making use of the application "press", so here is some clarification on it. CMC, with his emphasis on health taught press as a palm to palm position as in photo 91, whereas in the traditional Yang style it is a palm to forearm position as in photo 92. When using press in push hands, experiment with both so that you experience the benefits of each position. When pushing on your forearm, the location of the palm adjusts to the situation.

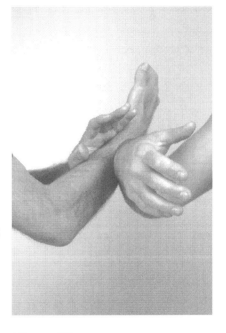

Photo 91

Photo 92

For more difficult forms like this it is helpful to have a little mnemonic ditty. This one goes: push, press, first rollback, second roll back.

This pattern has four versions, being pushed on the right and left ward off with each leg forward. When one person is being pushed on the right, the other is being pushed on the left. This creates advantages and disadvantages for each. It is generally easier to roll back towards our open side and harder across our forward leg.

When you are yielding with your rear leg ward off, the forward arm and hand can lightly coax your partner off balance by connecting with his/her upper arm and shoulder as you do the first roll back. Be cautious, for if you miss, your partner will have a great angle for pressing you through your open door. When you have the other arm up in ward off, the rear leg hand can't reach as far and will connect at your partner's elbow. Your leverage is not as good in this position, but it is still important to protect yourself from that elbow.

Be cautious of twisting the knees in this drill. Professor Cheng had a greater ability to open his kua and keep his knees stable than most of us, so trying to mimic his movements often leads to twisted knees. Remember to keep the weighted thigh and knee in alignment with the foot. For most people this also requires the navel to point the same direction as the weighted leg, so the range of one of the roll backs in this form will always be limited.

When you do the second roll back, do not pull or hook your partner's hands with yours. As you can see in photo 93 where I am hooking Brian with my right wrist, this creates tension in my wrist and is a "force against force" error. Generally people do this because they are afraid that if they just turn at the waist it will no be enough to draw the attack to the side of their center. Have faith! Neutralize by turning at the waist in response to your partner's attack. If done correctly, he will have no power left in the press by the time you transition to your push. Sometimes it is especially effective to do this rollback to the downward diagonal. Also try it with an upward diagonal.

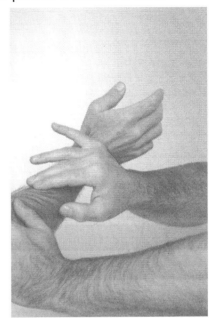

Photo 93

When you ward off, your intent is to protect your body by catching your partner's hands on your arm. When you push, your intent is to reach towards your partner's center – leave it to her to catch you on her arm. When you press, your intent is to triangulate back towards your partner's center, again leave it to her catch you on her arm.

Make sure that you yield judiciously. If you use up all your yielding room on the first roll back, you will have nowhere to go when pressed and will likely be knocked over. This is especially true when your first roll back is towards your rear leg. At times, you may be able to actually slip forward while doing the second roll back. Do this if it puts you in a more advantageous position. Joining and following a push does not always mean shifting your center back.

When you push, advance slowly and sense through your points of contact into your partner's rear foot. Take your time and really feel your partner. Compress your body down first into the rear leg and then transfer that compression to the forward leg. Imagine your energy pooling beneath your partner's feet as you advance. Advance with the body and keep the angles in your arms basically the same. Establish the structure of the arms and then move the momentum of the body forward through that structure. If you feel solidity in your partner, evaluate its nature and adjust your push accordingly. If you feel spacious yielding, evaluate that.

Many in this tradition are very soft. This works very well at advanced levels but can just be a manifestation of poor structure in less advanced players. If you get to push with someone like this, check if it works well for him. Pin his arms against his body and give him a nice strong push to his rear open door. If he topples easily, I'd take this as clear evidence that he is softer than his skill level merits. If, on the other hand, you land on your butt, push more with this person!

To achieve the proper level of softness, remember, the relaxation we seek in T'ai Chi is the maximum we can use and still get the job done. When you receive a push, at first you will need to brace enough in your body so that your partner's push is distinct and strong enough for you to effectively listen to and understand the push. If you move away too lightly, you will not get enough information and you will be easily pushed out. If this happens, go back to the immoveable ward off drill (page 81) to firm up your structure. As your skill improves continue to try to lighten up, but keep enough structure so that your body alignment is good and you can listen and understand effectively.

A comfortable place for the <u>change over</u> in this pattern is after the first roll back. Ideally, change overs should occur because one partner finds an opportunity to switch from yin to yang and attack. However, in the context of drilling, it is useful to cooperate about changing over. In this pattern, after the first rollback, the yin partner perceives an opportunity to switch to yang by pushing instead of yielding. This is similar to the simple two handed push hands pattern. In the example described above, after the first rollback, B switches to yang and pushes on A's right arm.

Practice all four versions of this form as a drill until it turns into a game. Then take time to double check your posture, your vectors, and that you are following all the fundamental rules of T'ai Chi and push hands.

Double Arm Ward Off Structure Drill:

<u>Time frame:</u> This drill focuses on building skill with a new position, where the forearms are both forward. The following couple patterns make use of this arm position, which is why we are drilling it first. It should only take you about 5 five minute sessions to build this skill enough to be able to use it in the more complicated patterns.

The position is similar to the common crossed arms position many people adopt when casually standing about, where the forearms are wrapped around each other, resting horizontally on the front of the body. In these forms, the forearms are away from the body, as high as the shoulder or a little lower. During the movement, one arm is in ward off and the other comes in to join and support it. It is useful to practice this movement by itself a little so that when it shows up in the forms you will be able to perform it easily. This movement is also called "elbow press" or "elbow smash" in later drills.

<u>Format:</u>
One way to drill this is to have one person stand in push, the other in ward off. Both stand in an enclosed stance. The pushing person remains in a comfortable and stable push of about ten pounds, neither shifting forward or back much. The ward off person practices starting with a right ward off (photo 94), then supporting that with the left (photo 95), then taking the right away leaving a left ward off (photo 96), then supporting the left with the right, then taking the left away and so forth. The movement of the arms arises from movements in the legs, kua, and pelvis that create a twisting motion back and forth through the waist and torso to the shoulder girdle. The weight should stay pretty consistent, not shifting back or forward much.

The supporting arm comes in as if to press, then the hand slides up the top of the forearm to the elbow, with the fingers and thumb going on top of the elbow (photo 95). The other hand first cradles the incoming elbow from the outside, then turns palm down to drop away as the incoming arm takes the full push. After the replacement has happened, continue turning to your limit in that direction, opening to the side. Then turn back and replace with the other forearm.

As the supporting forearm comes in, you can create more space for it by turning the arm already in place palm down.

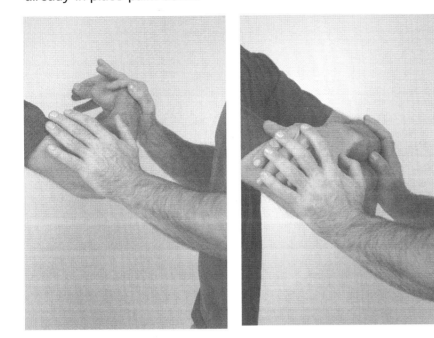 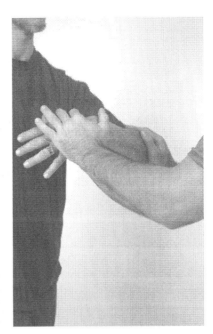

Photo 94   Photo 95   Photo 96

Do this twenty times and then hold a push for your partner so that he can do it twenty times. Switch legs and repeat.

You must get this motion fluid before going on to the next games.

Spiraling Upwards Ward Off Exploration:

Time frame: This exploration will take only a few minutes to understand if done carefully. You may benefit from returning to it for a few minutes several times. This is a movement we have not specifically studied before, but you have done it before. Polishing this skill will help you integrate it smoothly into the four hands patterns.

We are studying catching an incoming push on a ward off arm. The push is neutralized with a ward off that spirals it upwards if on the forward arm or to the side if on the rear arm. This exploration is choppy and does not flow smoothly from move to move.

This pattern has eight versions as you switch legs, arms and roles.
Time spent understanding the dynamics of this ward off in this small exploration will greatly improve your abilities in the more complex patterns coming up.

<u>Format:</u>

- Both stand in an enclosed stance with one person in a two handed push at the other's right wrist and elbow, that arm being in ward off. The "pushing" person is yang (B), weight back, while the "ward off" person is yin (A), weight forward (photo 97).

- Receiving the push and maintaining good peng structure, A neutralizes the push by spiraling the right arm upwards and a little to his right, fingers leading, shoulder attached to the spine and heavy, keeping the elbow down.

- Rewind the sequence back to the beginning, continuing to adhere, and do it again. B shifts a bit back, A a bit forward.

- Do the movements again. The yin person plays with changes in the arc of his rising ward off. The yang person maintains a solid pushing pressure, which should make it very clear to his partner the precise arc that his ward off must follow to deal with it! The yang partner seeks weaknesses in his partner's structure that he could exploit. The purpose of the exploration is to help the yielding person find an effective, well structured spiral.

Photo 97

Photo 98

In four hands (described a bit later), as this neutralization is complete, B would settle down to a push structure, right hand at A's right wrist. A, having had his left hand neutralized, would seek to continue coming in with his right forearm and elbow.

Once you have explored this way, switch arms maintaining the yin and yang roles. Now when the yin person does the neutralizing ward off, because it is his left arm, he does not need to spiral his arm as much upward and can neutralize more with a turn to his left (Brian is receiving this push on his left in photo 98). Again, in four hands, upon the neutralization, the yang push would change to a yang ward off/elbow attack and the yin ward off would change to a yin push structure.

The movement of the ward off is much more constrained when it is on the same side as the forward leg and must spiral upwards. When it is the same side as the rear leg, the ward off can move more freely. Notice this and take advantage of it.

Elbow Smash Game:

<u>Time frame:</u> This will take five minutes to understand (if you did the preceding drills!) and a few hours of practice to make smooth. Then you are free to play it as a game.

<u>Format:</u>
This is a pattern that makes most sense to me if it is understood as a variation on CMC's style. In this one, when the yang partner moves to press on his right wrist, his press does not connect adequately with his partner, so he slips his left pressing hand to the right elbow to bring the structure of his left elbow and shoulder forward. This ends up looking like a yang motion with both arms in a horizontal ward off structure at shoulder height. One ward off arm is forward of the other with the hand cupping back towards the other elbow. The other hand goes over the inside of the forward elbow, thumb on top. This can be called an "elbow press" or an "elbow smash" if referencing the incoming momentum of the second elbow.

- Both stand in an enclosed stance with A in a two handed push at the B's right wrist and elbow. B is in a right ward off with the left arm reaching forward for A's elbow with his left fingers (photo 99).

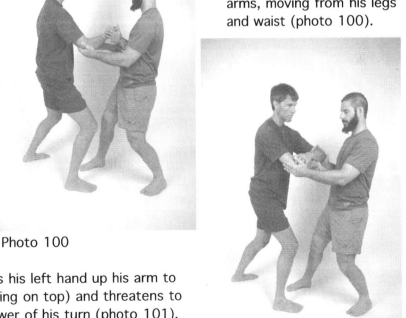

- A pushes, B yields and turns towards his right elbow ending up in a push structure on A's right forearm. B carries his arms, moving from his legs and waist (photo 100).

Photo 99

Photo 100

- As his push is neutralized to the side, A rolls the point at his right wrist and moves his left hand to press. Rather than completing the press, he slides his left hand up his arm to his elbow (hand and thumb going on top) and threatens to smash his partner with the power of his turn (photo 101). This motion allows A to re-center his attack and is very powerful, especially when going across the forward leg and closing that kua.

Photo 101

- B now has a two handed yin push structure catching A's two forearms. Yielding, B shifts back and turns to his left. He uses his right palm to protect from A's smashing left elbow.

His hands help roll the attack diagonally downward to his left.
- Having neutralized A's elbow smash, B switches to yang and comes in with a push. A rolls the point with his left hand with an upward spiraling ward off (photo 102), ending up in a yin push at B's left wrist with his right on B's left elbow (the mirror of photo 99).
- B comes in with his right arm to press/elbow smash, which A yields (in his yin push structure) to his right.

Here's the mnemonic ditty: push, press/elbow smash, first rollback, second roll back.

I mention the elbow <u>smash</u> to help you feel the power of the motion, but in the drill do not try to break or bruise your partner! As with any other drill, do it slowly, gently and with sensitivity. Collaborate on learning the flow and try not to break the drill by challenging your partner's balance. Once you have the flow, then you can separate yin and yang and start to challenge each other. If the pattern gets broken, stop and set it up carefully again.

Photo 102

This pattern has four versions, being pushed on the right and left ward off with each leg forward. When one person is being pushed on the right, the other is being pushed on the left. This creates advantages and disadvantages for each.

This sequence can change over between arms after the first roll back (the spiral upward) when the yin person switches to yang and comes forward with a two handed push. In the above example, after his first roll back, B would switch to yang and push forward on A's right forearm. Once you have cooperatively drilled the basics of this change over, see if you can do it by having the yin person choosing to go to yang (because he perceives the opportunity).

Martial Application   Variation:
This is a modification of the variation presented in Simple two handed push hands on page 81. The defender adds support of the elbow and attacking with it in response to the initial attack of pluck and split.

- Starting from the above example, as A pushes on B's right arm, B rolls back to his right towards the elbow of the ward off.

- B's right hand rolls the point to grasp A's right wrist and pulls it back and down to his right. Meanwhile he pushes against the back of A's right elbow with his left forearm or hand seeking to hyper-extend A's arm at the elbow (photo 103). Be gentle in the drill.

- A brings his left hand to his elbow to support it, prevent its hyperextension and to threaten B with either elbow (photo 104).
- B protects by catching both elbows with his palms in a defensive push structure.
- A rolls the point with his right wrist, and grasps B's right wrist in turn.
- Now A pulls B's right arm and threatens B's elbow with his left hand and arm.
- B supports his elbow with his left hand and threatens A with either elbow. And so on.
- Go back and forth, coordinating your weight shift with your arm movements to create power.

Photo 103

Photo 104

This approach makes the elbow smash drill even more intense. Grasping and twisting each other's arms can easily degenerate into force against force. Do your best to stay soft. Remember to practice listening even while executing a yang movement.

Practice all four hand and foot combinations of this variation.

Elbow Press Pattern – Wu Style:

This is the standard Wu style two handed push pattern as discussed in Master Ma's book.

As I mentioned earlier, Wu style push hands is typically done with a shorter, more upright stance than in Yang style, and as the weight is shifted back the toes of the empty foot are lifted. The waist and arm movements are just the same as in Yang style, but because of the postural changes in the legs, there is less distance to shift back and forth and thus waist turns are more subtle in Wu style. Rather than getting trapped into thinking that one is better, I suggest you experiment with both. All the drills in this workbook can be done in either type of posture. Often it is easiest to learn drills in the Yang style structure simply because there is more room to shift and turn.

This pattern is a more formal version of the elbow smash. Since there is less waist turn available in the Wu style structure, the double forearm structure shows up more as a simple forward push. This form has details in the hand rolling that are interesting and require sensitivity and coordination.

Format:
The yang motions are ward off and elbow press. The yin motions are roll back and push down.

- Both stand in an enclosed stance, the yang person (A) in a right ward off with the left arm reaching forward such that the left elbow/forearm is at the end of the right fingers. The yin person (B) receives in a push type structure with the left palm down against A's right elbow and the right palm up at A's right wrist. (Photo 105 shows this with roles reversed so you can see the hands more clearly. Brian has started to come towards me and both my hands are on the blades, in mid-rotation).

Photo 105

- A comes in with his yang ward off. B yields and turns towards his right. Both his hands rotate around the little finger (the blade of the hand) – right hand ends up palm down, left palm up. The arms are carried - they move only because the torso moves. Initiate the movement from the legs, pelvis and waist (photo 106).

- As his energy is neutralized to the side, A moves his left hand to press. Rather than completing the press, he slides his left hand up his arm to his elbow (hand and thumb going on top) doing an elbow press. This motion allows A to re-focus his attack (photo107).

Photo 106

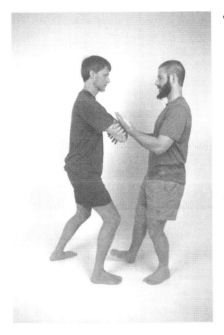

- Yielding before this second attack, B shifts back, turns to his left and presses down. B's hands help roll the attack diagonally downward to his left, left palm up, right palm down. Since this is Wu style, B's forward toe rises as he shifts back (photo 107).

Photo 107

- Now B switches to yang, and comes forward with his left hand. A turns this into a ward off shape which is caught by A in a push structure with right palm down at B's elbow and left palm up at B's wrist (photo 108). A will neutralize first by turning to his left, rolling both hands at the blade and then, once elbow pressed, by turning right and pushing down.

The ditty goes: "Advance with forearm, then elbow press; first roll back, second roll back, push down."

There are advantages to having one hand palm up and one palm down and to the sensitivity gained by allowing the hands to roll the point at the blades. Practice enough so that you able to use this.

Photo 108

This drill has four versions – two with each leg forward. By using the following change over, you can do both sides and then switch legs and do the other two.

Change over:
After doing the first roll back, if the yin person (B) senses a hole in the yang person's attack, he can switch to yang and advance with his right ward off. This switches the ward off arm for each partner.

In Master Ma's book, he presents thirteen "Basic Manipulations". These are variations of movement that might show up in a free exploration of this push hands pattern. Practicing these as drills will make them familiar and comfortable both to use and to respond to. Here is my articulation of one of these. I encourage you to peruse the original (although some of the language is hard to follow) and enjoy the photos of Master Ma pushing.

Elbow Tilting Drill:

This may be a little hard to figure out, so take your time.

- Stand in an enclosed stance with B in a right ward off with the left hand reaching for A's right elbow. A is in a push type structure with the left palm against B's right elbow and the right palm on B's right wrist (photo 109).

- B raises A's right elbow with his left palm (photo 110).

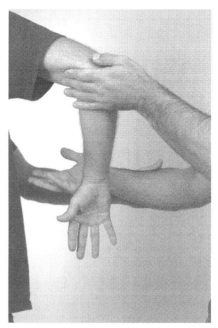

Photo 109

Photo 110

- A neutralizes by turning right through the waist and spiraling his elbow up, back and away from the lift. He reaches under with his left hand and replaces the point at his right elbow (photo 111). His right hand drops to cover B's left elbow.
  - B raises A's left elbow with his right palm (photo 112).
    - Again, A neutralizes by turning left through the waist, spiraling his elbow up, back and away from the lift. Becoming yang, he uses the turn to raise B's left elbow with his right hand (photo 113).

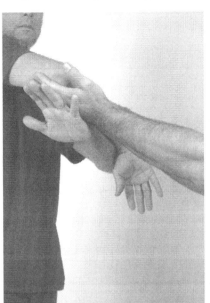
Photo 111

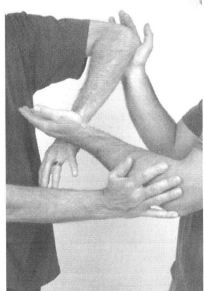
Photo 112

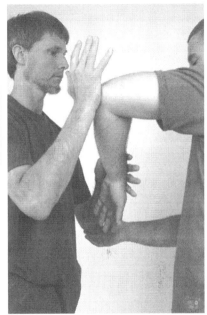
Photo 113

- B then does a first and second neutralization, and so on.

This has only two variations, depending on which foot is forward.

1/2 of Yang Style Four Hands Drill:

Time frame: This drill will take a few minutes to understand and only a couple hours of practice to make smooth. If it does not make clear sense, you are moving too quickly through these drills. Take your time and understand them in your body. Once you have this skill, integrate it smoothly into later drills.

This trains a part of the next two patterns. Instead of switching from yin to yang, one person practices each role repeatedly. For some people, this intermediate step can be invaluable for learning the sequence. Four hands is quite complex and difficult to learn without personal instruction. This drill makes it much easier. Despite this, some will try the complete four hands patterns first. If you do, please come back to this and the spiral ward off drill (page 91) to understand some of the details more clearly.

<u>Format:</u>
To do this drill, the weight shifts are minimized and the focus is on the twists in the waist (supported by opening and closing the kua) that support the arm movements.

- Set up in an enclosed stance with one person in a two handed push (B) at the other's right wrist and elbow, that arm being in ward off (A). The "pushing" person is yin while the "ward off" person is yang (photo 114).
- A comes **forward** and is rolled back in the direction of his fingers (his left) as B shifts back (turning to B's right).
- A then does press back towards B's center (photo 115).

- B rolls the press diagonally down to his left to neutralize it. As the press is neutralized, the pressing hand slips towards the elbow into a double ward off type structure (photo 116)

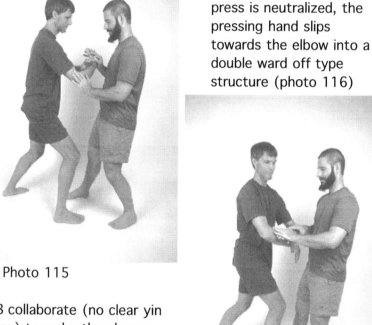

Photo 114

This part is just like a portion of four hands, which you will learn a little later. Now we do it again on the other side.

Photo 115

A & B collaborate (no clear yin or yang) to make the change over with the ward off arm so that now it is A's left ward off being caught by B's push. A should shift a little back, B a little forward. A has now switched sides (from photo 114 to 117)and the process is repeated on this side.

Photo 116

Photo 117

- A comes **forward** again and is rolled back in the direction of his fingers (his right) as B shifts back (turning left).
- * A then does press back towards B's center.

100

- B rolls the press diagonally down to his right to neutralize it. As the press is neutralized, A's pressing hand slips towards the elbow again into a double ward off type structure.
- Do the change over with the ward off arm again and now A comes in with the right ward off. And on.

This drill has four variations, one for each leg and each role. Practice this drill until it makes clear sense and is easy.

Four Hands, Reverse Timing

In this sequence, the push is yang, while the yin moves are a spiraling ward off and a double ward off. The distinct energies of roll back, press and ward off are not as clearly expressed as in CMC's or the forward timing version presented next. However, this sequence can feel very smooth. Structurally, this is the reverse timing of the formal Wu style described above and of four hands described next. Up until this point, when catching a yang push on a ward off forearm, we have always yielded towards the elbow, which is a natural drop. In this game, we practice yielding towards the fingertips as we just drilled.

Time frame: This will take a few minutes to understand and only a couple hours of practice to make smooth. Then it becomes a very rich game.

Format:
- Start in an enclosed stance with A in a two handed push at B's right wrist and elbow. B is in a right ward off with his left hand palm down near his left side (photo 118).

- A pushes, B yields and turns only slightly towards his left (towards the fingers of his ward off) as shown in photo 119.

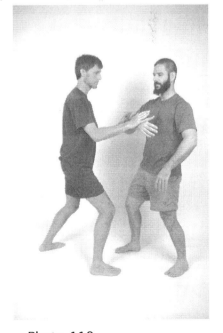

Photo 118

Photo 119

Photo 120

Photo 121

- A pushes back towards B's center. B brings his left arm in to a double ward off and does a second neutralization to his right (photo 120). This frees his right arm's elbow and allows that palm to turn down and the right arm to drop out.

- A continues to come in with his third push and B does a rising spiral ward off with his left arm, neutraliz-ing towards that elbow. In the spiral, A and B's same side wrists adhere (left to left in this case). B catches the last of A's energy in a push structure (photo 121).

- B has rolled the point at his left wrist by doing the spiral ward off with his left arm and he now settles down to a two handed push, becoming yang. B's left wrist connects with A's left, his right palm with A's left elbow (photo 122).

Photo 122

- A does a ward off with his left (towards the fingers of the ward off) for his first neutral-ization. B re-centers into a second push.
- A brings his right arm forward into a double ward off and does a second neutralization to his left.
- A rolls the point at his right wrist with a spiraling ward off with his right and moves to a two handed push, becoming yang. A's right palm connects with B's right wrist, his left with B's right elbow. And so on

Here's the mnemonic ditty: push three times, rollback then double roll back, spiral ward off and push.

Although in general the double ward off in this drill is yin, at some times it can be the transition point. If your partner does not catch the forearm of your second ward off, switch to yang and attack him with it. This will quickly train him to catch it!

In another variation, when I am yin, after I do the first neutralization, when I come in with the second ward off (my right), instead of being yang with the elbow, I can reach that hand towards my partner's belly. This threat causes my partner to take his right hand from my left elbow to catch my incoming right hand. I then drop my left hand and put it on his right elbow, roll the point with my right and do my first push.

This pattern is quite head on, with neither partner turning too far to either side. It is very similar to the "elbow smash" pattern, only it has three pushes instead of two. In some ways it is similar to the "over" change over in simple two hands, but there the yin person neutralizes by turning strongly to the finger side of the ward off and bringing the other arm over.

This pattern has four versions, being pushed on the right and left ward off with each leg forward. In this structure, when one person wards off with the right the other uses the left. This creates advantages and disadvantages for each person. The turns and angles are different for each version, so practice all four.

Once you have a good sense of flow going, drill the change overs. These generally take place when the weight is in the middle and the rising ward off is taking place. This would be where the yang person changes to yin. Instead, he insists on pushing three more times. In the example above, when B does his spiral ward off, I continue to push with my right hand on his left elbow. B neutralizes to his left fingers. A re-centers his second push, and B neutralizes to his left with a double ward off. He then does a spiral ward off with his right and settles to push. Simply switch from a yin rising ward off to a yang one hand push and reverse the direction. Your partner will now be doing a yin rising ward off. There is no change of hand position. Remember, the change should be initiated by the yang person because he feels a weakness in the defender's spiral ward off structure.

Four Hands, Formal Timing:

<u>Time frame:</u> This pattern is the culmination of your training to this point. It is the most difficult pattern and makes use of just about everything you have worked with in this book. If you have diligently practiced the preceding drills and games, this should come easily and make sense. If it doesn't, settle back to the games that are easier and work the four hands drills for awhile longer and then come back. This is a rich but challenging game.

<u>Format:</u>
This is the standard push hands structure in traditional Yang style and cycles through ward off, rollback, push and press (peng, lu, an, and ji) very clearly but in a different pattern than CMC's.

- Both stand in an enclosed stance with one person in a two handed push (B) at the other's right wrist and elbow (A), A's right arm being in ward off (photo 123).

- A comes **forward** and is rolled back in the direction of his fingers (his left). A re-focuses his attack with a press back towards B's center (photo 124).

Photo 123

Photo 124

- B rolls the press diagonally down to his left to neutralize it. He is now fully back. As A's press is neutralized, A's pressing hand slips towards the elbow into a double ward off type structure (photo 125).

Photo 125

- Having neutralized, B changes to yang and reaches with both hands towards A's center. Roles have now switched – A, who is now yielding protects himself by catching B's incoming hands on a spiraling upwards ward off with his left arm and rolls it to his left (photo 126).

- B reaches towards A's center with his left elbow but A catches the elbow in his right hand (photo 126).

Photo 126

- We have now completed a cycle –the roles are completely switched. B is now in a left ward off coming in to A's two handed push structure (photo 127).

- A rolls back the incoming push, B resolves to press, and A neutralizes by rolling it diagonally down.

Photo 127

The ditty for this pattern goes: "Pushing with hands, then forearm, then press; catch with rising ward off, then hands; neutralize the press down and go for the center!" Your clever partner defends by catching you on his rising ward off and on you go through the cycle.

As with the earlier patterns, spend plenty of time doing this as a drill, focusing on flow, collaboration, correct sequence and posture before trying to challenge each other. This sequence is very precise and somewhat angular, so take your time to get the structure correct and then work to smooth it out and eliminate force against force stiffness.

When you are learning this and practicing it as a drill, make sure that your contact is light enough to allow the transitions. This is quite a complicated pattern and there are many places where beginners get bound up. Go back to the two earlier drills on the 1/2 of four hands and the spiraling ward off to polish specific sections.

As with CMC's pattern, there are four versions of this, and each position has its strengths and weaknesses. Movements that feel spacious and strong when done with one arm may feel cramped and challenging at first with the other arm or foot forward. Work the challenging places to understand and strengthen your structure. Practicing this form will give you a physical understanding of the skills of ward off, roll back, push and press that will profoundly deepen your solo practice.

By staying clear in your intent when in the yang position, your partner will be forced to defend seriously. This will keep the form crisp and clean. Even as you become more experienced with this form, use the necessity of making your intent clear to keep the pattern to a moderate pace.

The change over is similar in feel to the easier ones I presented earlier. Again the yin person perceives a hole in the yang person's structure and switches to yang. In the above example, when A does his yin spiral ward off with his left arm, B does not come in with a strong left elbow, so when A catches the elbow he simply pushes forward with both hands on B's left arm. B then must neutralize to his left, A comes in with his left forearm and B then neutralizes to his lower right. This will teach your partner to come in solidly!

Hopefully, you have noticed by now that there is a pattern to how the four energies of ward off, roll back, push and press usually fit together.
- If push is yang, it will be caught by a yin ward off and rolled back to neutralize.
- If press is yang, it will be caught by a yin ward off and sandwiched down to neutralize.
- If ward off is yang, it will be caught by a yin push and rolled back to neutralize.
- If roll back is yang (as in helping the attacker to your rear with the forward arm in the CMC version above) it is redirected by a press.

Practice each of these two handed push hands structures until they have lost their drill – like nature and you are able to do the flow without thought. Then when you do free style push hands, you will find one pattern switching to another spontaneously. Be creative and put all the skills from the drills together into a very rich game.

Too few T'ai Chi practitioners are skillful at one of these patterns, and very few know them all. Going through the process of learning these forms as drills and making them fluid enough to be games will bring unanticipated rewards. Once you have done this, you will have developed an unconscious understanding of how to deal with hands reaching towards your center. Getting this physical coordination down allows you to really study the more difficult jings (skills) of T'ai Chi. It would, however, be possible to know all these drills and games and still have only a superficial understanding of the deeper skills. Therefore, use these games as a laboratory to study the masterful application of the skills (energies) of adhering/sticking, listening, understanding, receiving, neutralizing, ward-off, roll-back, press and push. These skills are based on awareness and sensitivity.

Congratulations on making it to this point in your training! If you have indeed developed competence in each of these drills, you should be feeling far more solid, flexible and sensitive than when you first started. You should have seen signs of the skills you have practiced physically showing up in the emotional push hands of relationships as well. I hope that this is helping you make your world into a place you can more deeply inhabit.

Although these games remain excellent training tools, it is only natural to take this into moving step push hands and the application of the diagonal skills (energies) of pluck, split, elbowing and shouldering. So when you are ready, step this way...

Chapter 8

Moving step patterns

In this section I introduce a few drills and games that involve moving the feet to make your self-defense skills more realistic. These include "moving step" push hands drills, a simple application drill from the form, a multi-step pattern called Da Lu (Big Roll Back) and basic circle walking from Bagua.

Once you have fixed step skills together, it's appropriate to make your drills and games a little more like fighting. Training in fixed step push hands can foster the impression that if you get mugged you should root and not move your feet. This is ridiculous.

What did the T'ai Chi player say to the mugger?
"Could you slow down your attack please?"

Or: "Hey, no fair, you moved your feet!"

If you ever have the misfortune of being physically attacked, your attacker will move quickly to gain a superior position. To defend yourself you will need effective footwork. Solo strength building forms have long deep stances. On the other hand, fighters move about with their feet beneath them. "Float like a butterfly, sting like a bee" - Muhammed Ali.

Fixed step drills can be modified to train footwork. Some drills are limited to taking a single step, some allow for multiple steps.

Clock Notation:

In order to talk about directions, I use the clock. Most T'ai Chi contexts I have worked in use directions with geographic words (North) or descriptions of the room (rear corner, front wall). I find the clock more versatile and useful (figure 12). The direction you are facing is your 12, your right is 3, your left 9, your rear 6. Corners are 1:30, 4:30, 7:30 and 10:30. This takes a little while to get used to, (and might challenge those of you from the digital age!) but the benefit is that it does not imply that we are actually stepping to the North as with the geographic descriptions and you can carry your 12 with you as you change your location or orientation.

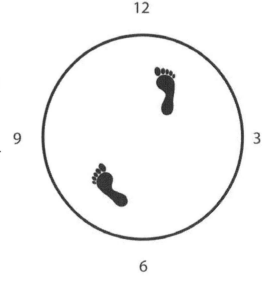

Figure 12

General Points on Stepping:

The reason to take a step is either that it makes you more comfortable or that it puts you into a better position. Stepping that endangers you or weakens your position is not helpful. We would like our footwork to support the principles of push hands:

- Maintain your own structure first!

- Stick to your partner, do not avoid or separate from her.

- Wait for her to initiate and follow her movement.

- Do not oppose or resist her movement, but by joining and following, gain a superior position (arrive first).

Before I present the drills themselves, here are some basic ideas about how to step in an actual fight. These skills are what the drills are designed to teach.

When attacked, step on a multiplication sign (X) not a plus sign (+)!

Stepping increases the opportunity to build momentum, so there are some guidelines for the direction you should step. If your partner attacks from 12 o'clock:
- Stepping to 12 is in direct conflict and is rarely a good idea.
- Stepping to 6 is on the line of his attack and may well just give him more room to build power and smash you.
- Stepping to 3 or 9 maintains the range and keeps you clearly visible – usually your partner will be able to adjust his attack effectively and hit you anyway.
- Stepping to the rear diagonals, 4:30 and 7:30, is a good strategy if you need space. It changes your angle, increases your distance and, if done properly, will put you in a superior position (or at least give you a moment to regroup). Do this when you feel scared.
- Stepping to the forward diagonals, 1:30 and 10:30, is a good strategy for moving in on your partner. If you can, do this. He will feel pressed as well as needing to change his targeting. Do this when you feel bold.

To repeat; when attacked, step on a multiplication sign (X) not a plus sign (+)!

It is safer for you if you step to the outside of your partner (his back). This makes it harder for him to reach you with his weapons. The downside is that he has fewer (though still ample) targets on his back.

It is more risky to step to the inside of your partner because he can reach you with his weapons. However, if well done, this makes his most vulnerable targets (eyes, throat, groin, knees) available to you.

On the other hand, when attacking step directly in and attack on a line. This builds your momentum and power. If you can, step in from your partner's diagonals. This makes it less likely that you will simply collide. If your partner is more massive than you, do not attack his body mass. Instead, attack his limbs or strike in a manner that slices through (his ribs, for example) allowing your momentum to continue.

Attacking the inside (from his forward open door) moves him back towards his rear open door as well as giving you lots of targets – but he can reach you easily with his weapons. This line will make it easier for you to knock him over, but also easier for him to move his rear leg to reset.

Attacking from the outside (across his forward leg) gives you fewer targets, makes it harder for him to reach you with his weapons and pushes him back towards his rear leg. This will make it harder for him to move his rear leg, and can force him to brace, which can make any blow you land more percussive.

The drills:
In order to train stepping in T'ai Chi, we start with single step drills. The most basic ones step straight forward and straight back because this is easiest. Recall, however, that stepping to your 6 when defending is generally foolish. Do drills like this to train foot agility and then move on in order not to build bad habits. The following drills are done with partners in an enclosed stance unless specified differently.

Attack: Step in with the rear foot as you push

Photo 128

The simplest step is just to allow your rear foot to follow you in when you push. This is a natural movement that will allow more of your momentum to be released into your push. This is especially useful if you are lifting in your push, and thus straightening your forward leg.

An easy way to drill this is to simply set up as in Pushing with a partner (page 63) with the "victim's" arms crossed on his body (photo 128). Push straight in to your partner's open door and step in with the rear foot so that once you have pushed your feet are essentially together (photo 129).

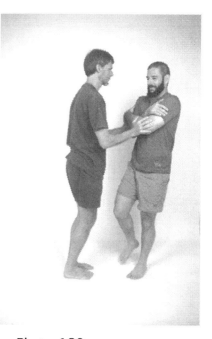

Photo 129

Your partner allows himself to be pushed out. It can be useful to push him towards a wall. You both may prefer to have the wall padded, although some teachers maintain that being pushed against a hard wall is beneficial.

You can also practice this in an uprooting format using the skills discussed on page 64.

An extension of this technique is to step through with the rear foot so that you end up in a forward stance with the rear foot now several feet forward of what used to be your front foot. You would only step in this way if you were convinced that you would be knocking the other person over, because during the time that you have one foot off the ground, you are quite vulnerable to being knocked over yourself. We will return to this stepping pattern again in a moment.

Once one person has been pushed over ten times, switch roles. Then switch legs. Do this drill for a few minutes each practice time until it is natural.

Attack: Step in with the front foot, then push:

The next natural step to practice is stepping in with the front foot immediately prior to pushing. Often once you have pushed, your rear foot will naturally step in. Allow that. As I mentioned earlier, this was a technique favored by Cheng Man-Ch'ing. By first stepping slightly forward, when you push, you come close to placing your center where your partner's used to be.

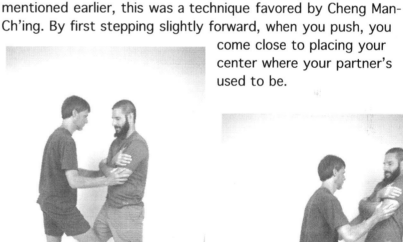

Photo 130

Drill this stepping pattern in the same manner as the last, playing with uprooting as well.

Photo 131

- Set up (photo 130).
- Step the forward foot in and prepare to uproot (photo 131).
- Push forward allowing the rear foot to come forward with the push (photo 132).

Photo 132

111

Take turns being tossed out. For this drill, remember to allow yourself to be pushed over. Once this drill and the last feel natural, agree with your partner to integrate them into your games so that when you have a clear opportunity to push, you step in and go for it.

This leads naturally to the next drills, which are **defensive** stepping patterns.

Defend: Step back with the front foot:

For the first level of this, imagine that the ball of your rear foot is nailed to the floor. As the push comes in, allow the whole body to pivot on the rear foot. This way, the body acts like a door that is being pushed open by your partner. The plan is that once he pushes open the door, he falls through it. Feel free to help him along!

In order for this to work, you must not consume all of your partner's momentum. This requires moving lightly just in front of the push and then, once your foot is placed, coaxing your partner slightly forward. If skillfully done, your movement will entice your partner to overextend forward, and a small tug or a push from behind will knock him off balance forward.

- At first, take the push on your crossed arms as shown in photo 133.
- As your partner pushes, allow him to push the right side of your body back, pivoting on the ball of the left foot (photo 134).

Once you have the pattern, try it in Simple Two Handed Push Hands with the forward arm in ward off. If you take the push on your right arm, you will be stepping back with your right foot. The angular change of stepping allows freedom for responsive movement with the right hand. Explore this a bit and we will come back to it in a few drills.

Photo 133

This step works best if the push is slightly off center towards the front foot, so when you are pushing, start by making this error obvious.

Photo 134

Once you have this movement, when you step your forward foot back, aim to step to the outside of 6 o'clock at an angle that gets you cleanly out of the way (towards a rear 45'), but keeps you close enough so that you are still adhering. To a

112

degree, the angle that your foot can retreat to is a function of how deep your partner's push is. In photo 134, Brian is giving me a shallow push, so my step is to 5. Were he to step in with his left foot with the push, this additional momentum would "push open the door" of my body more and I would pivot further on the ball of my left foot. On the other hand, if you step back and lose contact with your partner, this is your error, and does not place you in an advantageous position. In the flow of movement, once you have taken this step, you should adjust the angle and placement of your feet to a standard structure as soon as practical.

At first the leg will move like the pencil on a compass, drawing an arc around the fixed point of the rear foot. This throws some of your momentum out centrifugally. As the step becomes more comfortable, try to draw the arc of your leg through your center. In addition, as your comfort increases, have your partner push more directly on your center. This will make the whole process of your retreat more difficult.

Again, drill this for a few minutes each practice session with the focus now on the "victim" of the push. Make sure to do both legs.

Defend: Step aside with the rear foot:

If the push is more towards your rear foot, move that foot. Here the ball of the front foot is nailed to the floor and you pivot around it about 45' to the outside (to a rear 45'). Again, stay lightly in front of the push to entice your partner. Once you have stepped down, pull or push your partner lightly on his way.

- As with the last drill, first take the push on your crossed arms (photo 135).
- When the push comes in, step your rear foot to 6 to allow the push to go past (photo 136).

Once you have this flow, try it in Simple Two Handed Push Hands with a strong rear arm ward off structure. As you step back, use the forward arm to help your partner through the space you have just moved out of.

If you are pushing, push off center to the rear leg side at first to make it easier. As the

Photo 135

Photo 136

push comes closer to center, the defender must create a false sense of solidity to entice the push. When the push comes in, if you do not have enough room (provided by a well structured ward off), your partner will be able to pin you with his push and knock you out. This is true for both this and the earlier yin (defensive) step.

After you have drilled these two yin steps and the two yang steps above, you will have a fascinating place to study and train sensitive responsiveness in a very rapidly changing situation. Unfortunately, after doing one of these moves, you will usually have to reset, so it is not an endless flow.

These patterns, although more martially effective and sensible (in my view), are less common than stepping patterns that step to 6 o'clock. Here are those for both the yin and yang roles.

Attack and defend: Three steps to 6:

Often stepping drills are done where one person steps forward for a series of steps and then the roles switch and the other person steps forward. Often this is done in sets of threes to ensure that each person works each side. For the yang person, the focus is on being able to step solidly and to push continuously through the step. The yin person focuses on sensing and riding the push and rooting swiftly after stepping. As yang, you want to feel the opportunities and push through them. As yin, you want to stick and listen well enough so that you only step back when your partner steps forward.

This pattern is easiest to learn in Simple Two Handed Push Hands. Later you may want to also use it with other games. The yang person steps his rear foot forward into his partner's space with his push three times (an agreed upon odd number). Each step does not have to follow the last, he may choose to do a couple cycles of fixed step as he seeks a vulnerable opening. Once he has done three steps, the roles switch.

The yin person steps his forward foot back as the yang person steps in.

This is a pattern with no breaks, so it can build a good sense of cooperation and harmony.

At first, do this drill cooperatively, focusing on the points I mentioned above in your role as yin or yang. Once you and your partner are comfortable with this pattern, then agree to step through with your push at will. Once that is comfortable, agree to allow the yin person to step back to the diagonals. This will upset the flow of stepping to 6, but trains with more realism. If you step forward on your attack and your partner steps to her rear diagonal, move your feet as necessary to reset.

Now let's train some defensive patterns that use stepping forward. Remember, these express a bold and confident defense whereas stepping back expresses a more cautious or frightened response.

Defend: Step to the forward diagonal with the front foot:

When you are pushed, if you do not shift your weight back, eventually the push will equal your forward weight and your front foot will be free. I mentioned this earlier in the Immoveable ward off drill (page 44). When your foot is free you may be able to neutralize the push while at the same time stepping to your partner's outside with your forward foot. (You could also kick or knee him, but only do that with consent.)

This works well if you receive the push with your front arm in ward off (Brian in photo 137). Once the pressure is built up, neutralize it back and to your elbow as you step to the outside of your partner (to your forward diagonal) with the forward foot (photo 138).

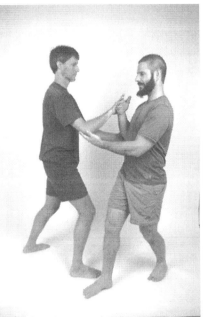

If your right leg is forward, step to 10:30 with the foot pointing that way (photo 139). This is an escaping maneuver and allows you to just keep going and get out of there!

Photo 137

Photo 138

Photo 139

If you want to stay and fight, step with the foot pointing to 1:30 (photo 140). Drop the rear knee and allow that foot to come up on the ball. This is a cross step related to bagua. Your momentum will support taking the next step around your partner's back with your left. Allow this.

Photo 140

Once you are behind him, use your hands to control your partner. If you were to strike, your right arm might clothesline him (upper arm to neck) or your left fist might naturally find his kidney. Or you might grab his throat with your left while hyper-extending his right elbow as I'm doing to Brian in photo 141.

Photo 141

If your rear arm is in ward off (photo 142), this pattern needs to be a bit different. Once the pressure of the push is built up, neutralize it to your elbow or fingers, bringing your other arm under to clear the push to your right as you step past it (photo 143). Your legs move in the same pattern as the first version. Step to the outside of your partner (to your forward diagonal) with your forward foot.

Photo 142

Photo 143

Explore follow up moves available after you step. Both these patterns put you in position to hyper-extend your partner's forward arm at the elbow.

To get more comfortable with the cross over type step shown in photo 140, practice it by itself. This is easy to do by starting in a horse stance (photo 144), then step to 9 o'clock with your right, moving it in front of the left leg (photo 145). The left knee drops, pointing to 9, and the heel comes up as you plant the right foot pointing as close to 12 as your knee allows. Then move the left foot to a horse again. Continue to your left. Then do it back to your right. Cross step, horse, cross step, horse. This step will be useful in later drills, so take the time to get comfortable with it.

Photo 144

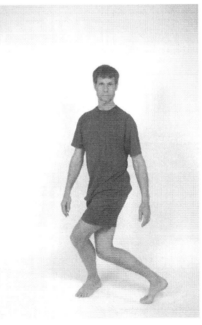

Photo 145

Defend: Step to the forward diagonal with the rear foot:

This is a similar structure to the last, but here you move the rear foot to the forward diagonal. At times you will not have the space to do so, which will require you to take a partial step back with the forward foot first. This description assumes that this is required, but only take that first step if you need it.

- A receives the push with a rear ward off (photo 146).
- A uses the compression of his partner's push to free up his front foot, moving it back a bit (photo 147).
- A yields to the left elbow as he steps his rear (left) foot to his forward right diagonal across his forward leg (photo 148). The rear arm does a spiraling ward off.

Photo 146

Photo 147

Photo 148

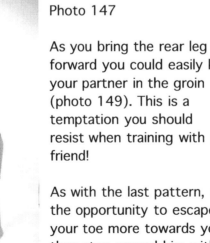

As you bring the rear leg forward you could easily knee your partner in the groin (photo 149). This is a temptation you should resist when training with a friend!

As with the last pattern, stepping strongly through gives you the opportunity to escape. If you want to stay and fight, point your toe more towards your partner with the first step and then step around him with your other foot. This will place you cleanly behind him, giving you rich opportunities for striking.

The other side of this pattern is described on the next page.

Photo 149

- A receives the push with a front ward off (photo 150).

  - A uses the compression of his partner's push to free up his front foot, moving it back a bit (photo 151).

    - A yields to the left fingers while the rear arm comes under (or over) and scrapes the push off at the wrist (photo 152).

Photo 150

Photo 151

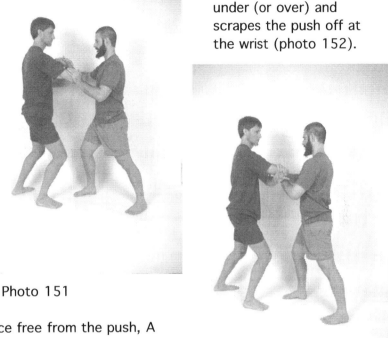

Photo 152

Once free from the push, A steps his rear (left) foot to his forward right diagonal across his forward leg (photo 153).

Practice the four versions of the stepping to the forward diagonal patterns with each leg forward and in the yin and yang role until they are easy for both you and your partner. After each execution you will need to reset.

Once you have these, integrate them into your games. As you add these kinds of steps in, the rules of interaction can become so open that the structure of the pattern falls apart with the enthusiasm of the moment. Do your best to maintain the forms. Continue to move slowly to stay with the principles and stay attentive to your posture.

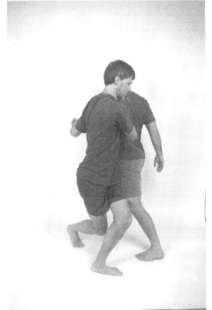

Photo 153

One step water drill

Here the pusher takes one step forward and the person being pushed one step back. This mimics an attacker stepping in and punching with the forward hand.

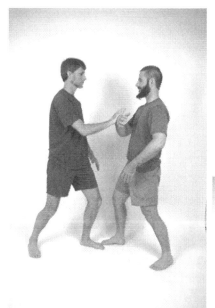

Photo 154

- Partners start in a mirror forward stance - one with the left foot forward, one with the right. Both use either the right or left arms, the hands touching at the wrist (photo 154).
- Using the right arms, the person with the left foot forward (A) steps forward with the right foot while pushing linearly to B's centerline (photo 155).
- B steps back (and a bit to the rear diagonal) with his right and rolls back (photo 155).
- Now the roles reverse and B steps through and attacks with his right, A steps back with his left and rolls back (photo 156).

Photo 155

Photo 156

Repeat, starting nice and slow, and if you like, building up speed and intensity. Keep the pressure between the hands light by yielding. Keep the attack linear. Re-establish the solidity of your stance after stepping by bracing your legs and maintaining "feet, legs and pelvis" alignment as you step back and forth. When you tire, use the other arm. For the left arm, the person with the right foot forward steps and pushes first.

Application drills:

Movements from the form can be used to create simple drills that train specific applications while working on footwork. Crompton's book, T'ai Chi for Two, is a good source for more of these, as is Wong's book and Yang, Jwing-Ming's Yang Style T'ai Chi Chuan. With a little thought, you will be able to devise your own. Here is an example:

Downward drag of Roll Back, Pluck and Split

When my partner pushes me, I may be able to do a roll back type movement while stepping back with my forward leg (this is "Step back with the front foot" described above). If done properly, this levers them down into the dirt (which can be very satisfying).

- Start in a same sided hip width right forward stance with B pushing on A's right ward off. A has his left arm forward to connect with B's right arm (photo 157).

Photo 157

Photo 158

- Because B's push is strong, A steps his right foot back to 7:30 while taking B's right wrist with his right hand and levering down on B's right elbow with his left forearm (photo 158). A brings his right hand close to this right hip and keeps it (and B's wrist) up. A presses down and sinks through his left forearm using B's arm as a lever to drive his face into the dirt. B's elbow is up so his arm gets locked in hyper-extension.
B, to avoid being levered into the dirt, yields to A's pull and steps forward with his right (photo 158).

Photo 159

- B brings his left foot in beside his right while dropping his right elbow and extending through his right fingers. This twists his hand from A's grasp and B in turn grabs A's right wrist with his right and A's right elbow with his left (photo 159).

121

- B pivots to face A and steps his right foot back to his new 7:30 (photo 160), dragging A to his forward open door and using A's right arm to lever A into the dirt (photo 160).

- A yields and steps forward with his right foot (photo 161) and the sequence continues as A takes B's role in photo 159.

Photo 160

Start this drill gently so that no one gets hurt. Once you have the pattern, speed it up a bit and stress each other's arms.

Photo 161

There is nothing like a nice strong yank to your open door to teach you how to yield to a pull! The yank is called "Pluck" (tsai jing) and refers to the jerk required to rip a feather out of a bird. Those of us who have not grown up plucking chickens, the action is a strong, abrupt jerk utilizing the sinking of the body. Here the power comes from stepping back and dropping your body to the rear.

The "Split" (lieh jing) is the attack at the elbow, hyper-extending it. If this is done abruptly and with power generated from an abrupt hip twist, you will damage your partner's arm. Don't. Instead apply it slowly to lever your partner down. Feel the potential, but allow him to twist out in order to continue the drill.

You should be able to get this pattern quickly (minutes), but stay with it to drill the dynamics of the stepping. Do a few minutes every session and this will become natural after seven times or so.

This drill can be done on both sides, so after your right arm is stretched out a little longer, do this with your left. Setting it up with the push at the start should make it clear to you that this is a valid response to a strong push when playing a moving step game.

Da Lu:

After learning moving step push hands and a variety of simple application sets, this is the next step of complexity. Da Lu means big roll back. Typical push hands works with the "front on" jings of ward off, roll back, press and push (peng, lu, ji and an). Da Lu trains the diagonal jings of elbow and shoulder strikes, pluck and split (zou, kao, tsai and lieh). Relatively few T'ai Chi players know these patterns. This is partially because the attacks are more dangerous and thus require greater care and training to use safely.

When receiving a push, as in the "drag" drill above, rolling back can lead easily into pluck. Plucking down on the wrist of an incoming elbow strike is also effective. Upon being plucked, a counter is to shoulder strike. This is defended with a split.

In Da Lu, we follow this sequence as a round – one person doing the yang, the other the yin and then switching roles. The steps and applications are done to the corners in essentially an X shape returning through the center again and again.

This pattern is best learned solo before practicing together.
For this description, the 12 o'clock remains stationary despite you moving about.

- Start with feet together facing 12, left palm on right in press (photo 162).

- Settling the arms with wrists still connected, step to 10:30 with the left foot. Drop the right forearm, extend through the left finger tips (photo 163).

Photo 162

Photo 163

- Step to 1:30 with the right into a forward stance and shoulder strike. The left hand is behind the right elbow, palm down (photo 164).
- Step the right foot back to touch heels with the left, the right hand rises by sinking the right elbow (photo 165).
- Pivot the left foot on the ball so the heel points to 10:30 (photo 166).

Photo 164

Photo 165

Photo 166

- Step behind with the right foot to 10:30 into a back weighted stance and roll back. The roll back turns into pluck down with the right and split with the left (photo 167).

Photo 167

- Step forward with the right foot beside the left and raise the right hand in a chop (photo 168).

- Step through to 4:30 with the left foot, dropping the arms.
- Step to 7:30 with the right into a forward stance and shoulder strike. The left hand rises to behind the right elbow, palm down (photo 169). And continue on.

Photo 168

Photo 169

The ditty goes, "Chop, step through, shoulder strike; step back, pivot, step behind, pluck and split." The chop, step through and shoulder strike are yang, the step back pivot, roll back (pluck and split) are yin. When the rollback turns into pluck and split, these are retreating yang movements.

As you do this solo starting facing 12, the shoulder strikes go to 1:30 and 7:30, the roll backs to 10:30 and 4:30. Pay attention to the solidity of your stance and keep your knees bent when your feet are together. If you like, you can put bricks on the ground to mark foot placement and step only on the bricks. Or if you want to be really thorough you could set posts in the ground that stand 8 feet above sharpened bamboo spikes. This will really make you pay attention. I have never felt the need to try this method!

This solo practice can be done on both sides, where the shoulder strikes would be done with the left shoulder and the left foot forward, the roll backs with the left leg back. When you do this with a partner, both of you will do right shoulder strikes. So to start, learn the solo pattern on the right and then practice it with your partner on the right side. Then learn it on the left and do that side with your partner.

This is what the pattern looks like with your partner:

- Both stand in press with the backs of their right palms against each other. A is facing 12 (photo 170).

Photo 170

- A, steps to 10:30 with his left. B pivots his left foot on the ball so the heel points to 1:30 (photo 171).

- A steps his right between B's feet to elbow strike him. B plucks down enough to straighten A's right arm as he steps back with his right foot to 1:30 (photo 171).

Photo 171

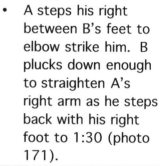

Photo 172

- A continues to come in with his shoulder strike. B settles into his back weighted stance and splits A's right arm with his left arm. This concludes A's attack (photo 172).

- B is now advancing yang. He steps with his right beside his left and chops to A's neck with his right hand. A sticks to B's right hand with his right and steps his right foot back beside his left (photo 173).

Photo 173

126

- B steps through to 7:30 with his left. A pivots his left foot on the ball to point his heel to 10:30 (photo 174).

    - B steps his right between A's feet to elbow strike him. A plucks down enough to straighten B's right arm as he steps back with his right foot to 10:30 (photo 175).
    - B continues to come in with a shoulder strike. A settles into his back weighted stance and splits B's right arm with his left arm. This concludes B's attack.

        - A is now advancing yang again and he steps with his right beside his left and chops to B's neck with his right hand. B sticks to A's right hand with his right and steps his right foot back beside his left (photo 176).

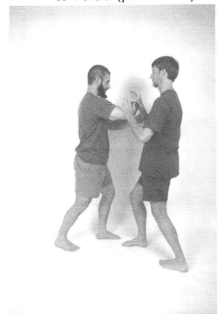

Photo 174

To get this flowing, cooperate at first to get the pattern and only then distinguish between yin and yang. Play it nice and slow with sensitivity.

Photo 175

When the yang person steps in to elbow and then shoulder, the yin person would like to step back a little to the outside (diagonal) of his line as discussed earlier. Further, he would like to put his foot down just after the yang person.

When the newly yang person comes in to chop, he can circle his right arm at his shoulder to break contact with his partner's right hand and chop, or choose to do a shorter faster straight on attack with the heel of palm. Just prior to this, he may be able to rock his partner's balance with his split to provide an opening for his attack.

Photo 176

After the yang person has been plucked and split, if his partner does not attack, he can continue his own attack by switching to the drag drill described above.

There are a number of variations of this drill, so do not be surprised when you meet them. Some versions emphasize the elbow strike more, some do not include it. Compton's has the left hand coming in to strike after the shoulder strike, which is then used by the partner as an opportunity to step in and push.

Once you have this pattern on one side, go back to the solo pattern to learn it on the other side. Then do that side as a partner drill as well.

When Da Lu is really comfortable, agree with your partner to explore other moves and applications as they appear. As you move to this freer form, expect to find yourselves falling into "force against force" errors. When this happens, slow down, breathe, relax and return to a more cooperative feeling drill.

Ba Gua:

Bagua is one of the three traditional internal Chinese martial arts (with T'ai Chi and Hsing-I). Bagua's forte is in its footwork. Even rudimentary practice of the circle walking and palm change drills can improve your footwork and understanding. To pursue this, find a teacher if you can. Here are a couple very simple drills that can add to your free stepping game. Bagua practitioners, please excuse me this simplistic presentation, I know there is much more to this practice than I present here.

Solo Circle Walking:

This pattern actually follows a figure 8 on its side – an infinity sign. When you do this, you are practicing walking around your opponent in each direction.

- Start in the middle of the infinity sign facing 12 and walk it to your left first, stepping your right foot pointing to 10:30 (photo 177).
    - Step the left foot to 9 (photo 178).

- And so on. The outside foot (the right here) will step to the corners (the diagonals) while the inside foot will step in the cardinal directions. You get 8 steps to go around the circle and then you are in the middle again, facing 12, left foot forawrd.
- Walk to your right now, stepping your right foot pointing to 1:30.
- The inside foot (the right now) takes the corners (the

Photo 177   Photo 178

128

diagonals) while the outside foot points to the cardinal directions. You get 8 steps to go around the circle and then you are in the middle again, facing 12. Although this description is of the right foot stepping to the diagonals each time, the fundamental movement dynamics are the same whether you step diagonal with either foot. Because you stepped first with the right, it goes to the diagonals. You could just as easily step with the left first as well. Just be consistent in which foot goes to the diagonals and which to the cardinal directions..

Walk this circle to train footwork. Speed up once you have it. Ancient masters are reputed to have run these circles so fast their queues would be horizontal behind them.

Keep your navel generally pointing on the curve of the circle while extending the inside arm towards the center, the rear hand covers near the inside shoulder. Sit the wrists. You will need to transition the arms from rest when you start and from right to left as you switch circles in the cross of the figure eight.

Once you can walk the circles easily, do a cross over step (as practiced earlier) in the middle of a circle and switch directions. If walking around with your left shoulder inside (photo 179), and we call the center 12, step with your right foot to 10:30, bringing your right hand up under your left arm so it ends up reaching to the center of the new circle while the left covers (photo 180).

Photo 179

Photo 180

After you can do the solo circling easily, and do the cross over steps in both directions with the hand changes, you are ready to practice this with your partner.

Partner circle walking:

This drill will teach you how to walk around your partner and leads into free stepping games. There are similar drills with swords.

- Partners stand on opposite sides of the circle with their right arms connected at the wrists (photo 181).

Photo 181

Photo 182

- Each steps the right foot clockwise around the circle. The navel points on the curve of the circle, the left hand covers, head turned to look at your partner. Each partner tries to walk around the other. The effect of this is that each walks around the same clockwise circle with the point of contact in the center (photo 182).

Once you have the hang of this, cross step to 10:30 (assuming the center of the circle is 12) with your left foot and switch hands, bringing the left forward under the right. Your partner should cross step in response out of self-protection. Get this going cooperatively so that it is fun and easy.

Then up the ante. Cross step and swipe at your partner's kidney or belly as you go by (photo 183). In the above pattern, the cross step and the swipe would be with the left (going left to right with the momentum of your step). Do an open handed swipe so that if you connect it will only be a slap. Keep the tempo slow and friendly to avoid injuries, grumpiness and brawling.

Now if you like, you can combine the circle walking with the stepping patterns you learned earlier. No doubt you can see how Stepping to the forward diagonal with the front foot (page 115) is an adaptation of the cross step and circle walking.

Photo 183

Free stepping play:

At this point, train to be able to step freely and creatively as you play. Root solidly after stepping (immediately brace your legs!) Agree on rules that keep you safe. Start in a push hands format. Only step to make yourself more comfortable or to gain a superior position. Work to keep the tempo leisurely. If you are going to allow striking of any kind, train your control so that you can freely strike knowing that you will not injure your partner (see below for some training tips).

Often it is helpful to designate one person the attacker while the other defends. Imagine a scenario where it would make sense for the defender to not simply run away. If you are defending, adapt to the person's attack. Look for places to use your circle walking skills.

To make your play still more realistic, vary the style of attack (punches, kicks, grappling, drunken) while still keeping the tempo down. Explore responses and look for ways to use form applications and push hands skills.

Some martial arts styles train at a far distance where the weapons are kicks and extended punches (Tae Kwon Do, for instance). This kind of fighter will come into range, try to hit you, and then retreat out of range. How can you adapt your skills to this kind of attack? Can you wound the limbs? Can you enter in and control your partner's balance as he is reaching for you with fist or foot?

Other styles (eg. Jujitsu) focus on grappling, locks and throws. What are you going to do if someone tries to tackle you, dives for your legs or tries to get you in a lock? Although push hands focuses on pushing for safety reasons, that same energy can be put into a strike. Striking a grappler may be the most effective way to keep him at a distance. I weigh 150 pounds. Allowing a 250 pound grappler to close with me would not be a wise strategy.

In closing, I'll just touch on a few topics.

Striking vs. pushing:

We push in many of these drills because it is less dangerous, but also because in T'ai Chi we wish to reduce violent conflict, not contribute to it. The hope is that after being pushed down an attacker would have a moment to reconsider. Recognize that this is very kind to your attacker. You may not be feeling that charitable, and you may not think it wise to allow him to regroup. Thus, from a self-defense perspective, it might be wise to strike and incapacitate an attacker. Or to push him in a way that knocks him into something hard. Walls, the ground, drinking fountains and cars may be convenient things to push him into and this protects your hands from the impact of striking. Generally, if you have the skills to push an attacker out, you also have the skills to hit him while you're at it. In fact, it might be wise to hit him first and then, while he's in shock, to push him away.

Whole Body Fist:

As your skills improve, it is important to understand how to press your attack with whatever part of your body is available. This is called whole body fist and includes skills for using your:

Knees and thighs – of course you can knee into someone's stomach, groin or thigh, but you can also use your knees and thighs to rock your partner's balance when your legs are close enough. There are many situations in fixed step push hands where the knee and thigh can be used to help unsettle your partner. If you want to do this it is polite to agree to it first.

Hips - If you are close enough, you can use your hips to deliver an unbalancing push or a blow.

Elbows and shoulders – Da Lu is a good way to start to train these. These are very good close quarter weapons. Explore the range of motion of the upper arm at the shoulder to feel the possibilities for striking with the elbow to the front, side and back.

Head – the head can be used to butt with the forehead. If you do this, make sure you hit something softer than your head. Head butting someone else's forehead would hurt, but squashing his nose would be softer. In push hands, a slight feint with the head should be enough to alert your partner to this danger.

Kicking – This is hard to train in a push hands structure. Generally, T'ai Chi kicks are low and a good rule is to only kick when three feet are on the ground – one of yours and both of your partner's. The only way to ensure that his feet are on the ground is to control his balance as you kick. If he is struggling to stay upright he will not be able to defend against your kick. If he does have control of his balance, your kick may well be caught and used to knock you on your butt. A good way to train your feet is sticky feet from Wing Chun, where each person has one foot in contact with the other's and circles much like in one handed pushing. Hacky sack is also a useful foot training game.

High kicks with targets to the head and fancy spinning kicks are generally not part of T'ai Chi arsenal because they are designed for a longer distance art and they leave you open for longer.

Conditioning for striking: if you are interested in being able to strike, it is useful to condition your weapons. This is done by hitting things. The effect of this is to harden your weapon, to train your body both how to hit with this weapon and to learn how sturdy it is. The last two benefits should not be underestimated as, if educated, your body will instinctively only hit as hard as the weapon can withstand. It is unwise to hit someone so hard you break your wrist.

There are a number of tools that can be used for this kind of conditioning, ranging from hitting or kicking heavy bags, makiwara, trees and iron plates to driving the fingers through hot sand or pebbles. Personally. I am very careful of my hands because I like to play the piano and make pottery.

Conditioning for being struck: if you ever really fight, you will probably be hit. So although must of us train to avoid blows (and fights), fighters must also train to withstand blows. There are many accounts of skilled T'ai Chi players being able to take blows (William C.C. Chen, for example). Iron Shirt Qigong is a text by Mantak Chia which describes systematic training for this ability.

San Shou

After learning moving step and da lu, it is appropriate to study San Shou, a complex sequence of interlocking forms that train a wide variety of defensive and offensive moves. There are several san shou forms taught by different teachers. Due to their complexity, these are best learned directly from a knowledgeable instructor. Jonathan Russell describes a pattern taught by T.T. Liang in – The T'ai Chi Two-Person Dance.

Chin Na, Grappling and Throwing:

Chin na is the art of locking the joints in order to control your partner. This is an entire realm of study. Most martial arts include some of these skills. Some push hands structures lend themselves to setting the opponents up for a nice chin na application. This material is very difficult to learn without getting a "feel" for it. I recommend you study this with a qualified instructor. Yang Jwing-Ming has some good books and videos on this.

There are many grappling and throwing applications in T'ai Chi. Again these are best learned with a mat and a qualified instructor. If you have the passion for this, find someone to learn from. Although JuiJitsu, Aikido and other arts have great skills in this regard, it is best if you can find a T'ai Chi instructor who knows this material so that you do not have to adapt to a new art.

Weapons For Two:

There are two person drills for saber, sword, staff and spear that are very useful for training some of the same skills we have been working on here. If you have the opportunity, I recommend studying these with a qualified instructor. Becoming able to stick/adhere, listen and understand with an eight foot staff or a sword will make your empty handed work that much more sensitive.

Contact Improvisation (CI):

This is a dance form that shares interesting skills with push hands. Those of you who do partner dances (that involve physical contact) like ballroom, swing, contra and square dancing, have probably applied T'ai Chi skills to dancing already. CI is a form that involves providing support for one another through the point of contact in order to explore and improvise movement. Here, rather than understanding your partner's center in order to control it and hurl them across the room, you seek to understand it in order to create collaborative beauty and interest. If dance appeals to you, I highly recommend exploring this form with a local group.

****

The skills we have worked on here are the foundation of good interactive T'ai Chi. Regular practice with other serious and open minded students will develop your skills. It is also a good idea to push with new people from time to time. Be prepared for differences in understanding and make sure that you agree on the rules and intent before you play. It is no fun to push with someone who thinks that stepping in and striking is OK when you thought you were going to do nice slow fixed step!

Be aware that there are more advanced skills. These become increasingly difficult to learn without the modeling and energy transmission from a qualified teacher. If you are interested in progressing further, find a teacher locally or go to workshops. Subscribe to magazines, read books, study videos and search the internet. There is so much more material available than when I started in 1978! Take advantage of it.

Congratulations on making it through all those explorations, drills and games! If you have really learned them, you know more than most other T'ai Chi practitioners about two person patterns and will be able to play with people from other styles than your own relatively easily. Most of all, enjoy all aspects of your T'ai Chi practice and find ways to make this world one you want to live in.

Appendix   A

Learning   How   To   Relax

One can say that the first principle in T'ai Chi is to relax. This is functional relaxation, which means that the goal is to relax as much as possible while still getting the job done. The soft flowing motion of solo T'ai Chi requires relaxation, as does the responsiveness of partner work.

Despite this being so fundamental to our practice of T'ai Chi, more attention could be given to the logistics of how to actually accomplish this (other than simply practicing the form).

Functionally, relaxation is experienced as soft, pliable, mobility in the joints. All skeletal muscles are designed to produce movement in joints. If a joint remains in a static position, this starts to impede blood flow and stiffen the muscles that control that joint. If a muscle is tight, this limits motion in the joint, decreasing blood flow and creating stiffness. Over time, tension and stiffness can become chronic leading to constriction in the fascia (the connective tissue sheath surrounding our muscles and joints),

It is relatively straightforward to learn to relax, but it takes attention and repetition and is not easy. The first aspect is learning how to physically relax. The second is to understand the emotional and cognitive issues (from your past, present or future) that cause tension. The third is to understand the environmental and usage issues that lead to tension. This appendix focuses on physical relaxation, but let's look at each of these in turn.

Physical   relaxation:

To relax your body on purpose, you need to know how to give your muscles the correct signal. Many people try to relax by using their will. This is not terribly effective, since muscles, by the nature of their fundamental structure, respond to a direct request by tightening.

Example: Take an arm, and while at rest, send nerve impulses to your bicep that will make it relax. Not real effective, eh?

On the other hand, here are five ways to effectively relax a muscle. Different techniques are useful at different times.

1) Tense the antagonist muscle to move the joint.
2) Tense it first, so that it is relieved to relax.
3) Visualize and imagine sensations of warmth, flow, melting etc. in the muscle.
4) Allow the joint to be moved by a source other than that muscle.
5) Get a great massage.

Explorations:

1) Contract the biceps of one arm so that your hand moves towards your shoulder, flexing the elbow joint. This relaxes the triceps on the back of the upper arm. Muscles have resting tone,

so if you massage your triceps it will probably still have some stringiness to it. If you do an isometric contraction of the elbow (as weight lifters do to show off the biceps), keeping the elbow stationary, this tenses both the biceps and the triceps. If you try to lift an object that is too heavy for the biceps (I'm trying to lift my desk, for instance), you can hold a strong contraction of the biceps and relaxation of the triceps. If you try to extend your arm against a barrier, this will tense the triceps and relax the biceps.

This is very useful in the following kind of situation. Many people have lower back pain from time to time. Often this is due to a muscle spasm in the muscles on either side of the spine in the back. These muscles have tightened (usually to prevent or splint an injury) and are scared to let go. Gentle contractions of the abdominal muscles (forcing the back muscles to relax) can often ease this quite quickly. To use this therapeutically, only do 5% of the motion available in the joint with as little power as possible. Micromotion is the target. Feldenkrais movements often take advantage of these principles.

2) Systematic, whole body relaxation based on the tense and release strategy is standard in stress management. Usually this is done lying down and your back. Once you are comfortable, tighten the entire right leg so that it rises off the floor, hold it for as long as you can without straining. Then release. Take an intervening breath. Then tense the other leg in the same fashion. Take an intervening breath. Tense the buttocks. Then tense one arm, then the next. Tense the trunk. Tense the neck and face. Finally, tense the whole body, squeezing all the remaining tension out. And release! Allow the whole body to rest, melting into the floor, allowing the breath to deepen and soften.

This is a very useful exercise for letting go of pent up tension and the physical effects of distressing emotion.

3) Visualizations of warmth, tingling or blood flow or simply paying attention to the perceptions coming in from the nerve endings in a given area will often relax that area. Give this a try by feeling your right foot from the inside out. Imagine that your foot is relaxing in a deeply pleasurable way. As it relaxes, you might be feeling a sense of warmth or melting. You might be feeling each individual toe relaxing, letting go, and melting into the floor. Big toe, index, middle, ring and little toes each relaxing out to the toe nail. The surface of the skin might tingle as you relax even more, bringing a sense of aliveness out to the sole of the foot and the small hairs of the skin. You might notice a sense of aliveness permeating the very bones of your foot and toes. Allow your awareness to travel through your foot like a glowing spotlight of warmth and caring, sensing into small places in your foot. Take some deep breaths and just enjoy these sensations, relaxing a little more.

Just reading this can be deeply relaxing for your foot, but if you take the time to give your right foot your complete attention, the effect will be far more powerful.

Standing meditations, moving chi kungs, solo form and partner T'ai Chi make use of this principle, using visualization, imagination and attention to create relaxation. This is a skill that can benefit from drilled practice where this is the sole focus. This is best done lying down.

4) It can be very effective to use an external source to move a joint. A fun way to do this is to have a friend take your arm as you are standing, and move it gently through its range of motion. Holding and supporting your arm, your friend creates movement that you simply allow by releasing your arm joints. With practice, you can learn to totally relax your arm. This is maximum looseness and very relaxed. You may find it challenging to completely release your arm. Allow yourself to be curious about that (as opposed to judging yourself for not getting it faster) and learn something from it.

If you allow it, this exercise can be quite emotionally evocative. Most of us have issues around trust and letting go, and they may surface through these exercises. Be gentle with yourself and make space for this aspect of your experience also.

Shaking chi kungs make use of this principle by using one part of the body to create a movement that can allow other parts to relax. By bouncing in my legs, I can create an opportunity for my shoulders, arms and jaw to relax.

On a more subtle level, the diaphragm and the heart are constantly creating motion that we can use to relax the body.

A good way to experience this is to lie on the back with the knees bent and the feet on the floor. Take a little of the weight of the pelvis onto the feet by pushing with five to ten pounds against the floor. Don't lift the pelvis off the floor, just take some of its weight so that the pelvis can move more freely at the articulations at hips and spine.

Take some very deep and relaxed breaths and notice how this moves the pelvis. Inhale deeply – how does the pelvis move? Exhale deeply, how does the pelvis move with that?

For most people, in relaxed, normal, breathing (as opposed to either shallow or reverse breathing) the pelvis will tilt up towards the sky and shoulders (flexing at the spine) on a complete exhale and will extend at the spine, arching the back a bit, on the inhale. (This movement is described as having two parts – it is actually more complicated. Use your attention and study what is true for you.)

This movement is used in standing and sitting meditations to keep the joints mobile. Doing so requires a deep level of allowing. Once you have a clearer experience of this standing, you can bring this to your form practice (where it will change if you are doing reverse breathing).

Movement induced by the heart beat can be experienced when sitting with one thigh over the other. If the top leg is loose, it will move with the heart beat. How can you make use of this to deepen your relaxation in your standing meditation and form practice?

5) When was the last time you had a great massage? Swedish styles increase blood flow through the body to allow the muscles to release toxins and rest. Trager uses motion and traction by the therapist to allow you to release the joints. Deep tissue styles release constrictions in the fascia allowing greater range of motion and freedom. Acupressure based styles balance the energy flows throughout the body.

Often we have tension and limits in our range of motion that are very difficult to release without help. Give yourself the gift of good bodywork.

Emotional and cognitive issues that cause tension.

We are all familiar with the way that emotional distress and disturbing thinking can lead to physical tension. Most often, the source of this stress is either in the past or the future and only rarely in the present. There are, of course, the moments when we are actually experiencing painful things. However, most of us are blessed and are not in dangerous pain right now, thank goodness.

Most of the distress we feel is either residual distress from past pain, or worry about pain we may experience in the future. It can be deeply relaxing to:
1) Release pain from the past.
2) Drop worries of the future.
3) Practice paying attention to the present moment.

Past pain can be released by facing it and digesting it. We want no hidden skeletons in our closets, and we want to have processed our history enough so that we can honestly tell ourselves that there is no longer any need to dwell on it. Until we have acknowledged what our past was, understood how it has effected us, and learned whatever we can glean from it, we will not want to really let it go.

Many people can benefit a great deal from autobiographical reflection and journaling. This process may not be all you need if you have had a difficult history. Fortunately, that is what psychotherapy is for.

Worries of the future sometimes arise because there are things that you can do to prevent future hardship. These are cues to plan for the future and to take action now. On the other hand, many worries about the future are about things over which we have no control (loss and death, for instance). As with our past pain, these worries need to be processed enough so that we can honestly tell ourselves that there is no longer any need to dwell on them. Only after we have acknowledged and reflected upon our worries we will be able to let them go.

Paying attention to the present moment is a habit that is built over time. Form practice and partner work are wonderful ways to train this. This is a benefit to making your form so precise and multilayered that you make errors if you are not in the moment. As you advance, your precision and depth in form practice should keep pace. In partner work too, it is important to work with drills and partners who are sufficiently challenging so that you get instant feedback when you are not present. There's nothing like the danger of getting knocked over or hit to focus the mind in the present!

When not doing T'ai Chi, it can be useful to remember that you can tell where your attention is by the contents of your awareness. Physical sensations and perceptions occur in the present. Anything else, including thoughts, memories, and worries does not. As I mentioned above, for most of us, most of the time, the present is pain free (and may even be joyous!). So keep your mind relaxed by reducing the distracting charge of the past and the future and keeping your attention on the present.

Environmental and usage issues that lead to tension.

As we refine our understanding of our own tension, it becomes necessary to look at our lifestyle and consider the effects that issues such as diet, exercise, sleep, social contact, sexual habits, posture, body use, and overall life satisfaction have on our sense of peace. In terms of this, it would be very helpful if the body came with a user's manual detailing the ideals for each of these! Without this, we are thrown back on our own ability to perceive what is most nourishing for ourselves in each moment. To make things more difficult, this is likely to change from day to day. Persistent attention will teach you what generally works best for you. Consistent practice of the form is a great way to do a daily check in with yourself. Over time, you will discern patterns and preferences. Many of these are genetic or a reflection of your temperment and are your personal manifestation of the Tao.

Study them and use this as an opportunity to flow with the Tao. As you become more responsive to what is true about you (as opposed to what you thought or hoped was true) you will naturally feel more relaxed and at peace. For instance, caring for your body by giving yourself enough sleep or protein or being attentive to your posture will naturally make you calmer than willfully deciding to sleep four hours a night, subsist on raw carrots and stand with your head bowed.

Conclusion:

Understanding how to relax allows us to manifest this central principle more in our T'ai Chi practice. There are specific things that we can do to relax physically and psychologically and to respond to the needs and preferences of our precious human body. It is relatively straightforward to learn to relax, but it takes correct effort applied with consistence to become skillful. I hope that you have found some approaches in this appendix that you will apply in your life to cultivate greater peace and relaxation and that this will contribute to your life and T'ai Chi practice in a meaningful way.

Appendix B

Understanding   Physical   Self Defense

Everyone wants to stay safe. To help you do that, you need to understand the dangers and what specific actions to take to protect yourself.

Understanding   the risk:

Here are some disturbing statistics from the CDC and Dept. of Justice:

- .2% of Americans over 12 reported being physically assaulted in 2005. Twice as many males reported being assaulted than females.

- .08% of Americans over 12 reported being sexually assaulted or raped in 2005. Ten times as many females reported being assaulted than males.

- Those under 25 are victimized almost twice as often as those older.

- 17% of women and 3% of men reported being victims of attempted or completed rape during their lives.

- 29% of women and 22% of men reported experiencing physical, sexual or psychological violence by their intimate partner during their life time.

- 9% of high school students (11.9% of girls and 6.1% of boys) reported being forced to have sexual intercourse.

- 20 – 25% of college women reported experiencing completed or attempted rape.

- 57% of rapes happen on dates.

- 73% of sexual assaults are by known perpetrators – 38% friends and acquaintances, 28% intimate partners and 7% other relatives.

- **However,** there has been a very significant (50% !) decline in physical and sexual assault in the last ten years.

Women are slightly more likely to be physically assaulted than sexually assaulted, and are most at risk younger than 25. The assailant is most likely (70%) to be known.

Men are much more likely to be physically assaulted than sexually, are most at risk younger than 30, and the assailant is most likely (60%) to be a stranger.

Now that we better understand the risk, what can we do to protect ourselves?

Traditional T'ai Chi writings are boiled down to the essence. In contrast, typical writings in the modern U.S. are padded to respond to the assumption that longer books are more valuable. If length is important to you, make 30 copies of this and staple them together! If not, simply read this enough times so that you could explain it to your daughter.

The next paragraph is my summary of the T'ai Chi attitude towards self-defense. Understand it deeply and internalize it in your own words.

The attitude:
The highest level of self-defense is preventing violence and preserving life. Assess yourself and others honestly and correctly in terms of 1) respect for others and 2) self-control. Respect the four factors that undermine self-control. Limit the opportunity and means others have to hurt you in order to preserve your safety. Do not be at the point of conflict. If you find yourself there, avoid first, deflect second and only counter when necessary.

Unpacking the attitude:

Many people who are drawn to the martial arts are interested in realistic self-defense. This is usually less true for most people who practice T'ai Chi Chuan despite its roots as a martial art. However, effective self-defense is still part of the curriculum.

In self-defense, the moral high ground, and thus the position with the most power, is to be concerned not only with protecting your own body, your loved ones, your goods, needs and preferences, but also with creating a world where everyone is treated with respect, understanding and compassion. Thus we dedicate ourselves to preventing damaging conflict and violence, and to preserving life.

One important rule in self-defense is: Don't Be At The Point Of Conflict. This applies to not being at the end of your opponent's punch, not being in a bar in the wrong part of town and choosing your friends and associates wisely.

In order to not be at the point of conflict, we must understand the types of attacks and the types of assailants.

Attacks come in forms ranging from bacterial, to verbal, to full out physical assaults. The principals of defense remain the same in each case, but are adapted to the unique situation. In this appendix I will only address physical assault. We will discuss types of attacks more in a moment.

Assailants range on continuums of selfishness and poor self-control from every-day people in a bad mood to chronically selfish and out of control people. For the first, the attack is usually quite personal and based on a perceived slight or offense on your part. For the latter, you are simply an available victim.

Assailants require increasing levels of disincentive to prevent or terminate an assault as they are more selfish and/or more out of control or committed to violence. Most people might just need a little space and understanding to reconnect with their habitual respect for others. Mildly selfish people need to understand that their misbehavior will have long-term negative consequences for them. The habitually selfish and/or out of control may need to be physically prevented from perpetrating an assault.

"If you know others and know yourself, you will not be imperiled in a hundred battles;... if you do not know others and do not know yourself, you will be imperiled in every single battle." Sun Tzu, The Art of War, T. Cleary Trans.

The T'ai Chi approach to self-defense emphasizes knowing ourselves and awareness of others and our surroundings. This is what allows us to assess the safety of a given situation and to choose to not be there. Or, if we find ourselves there, our awareness allows us to respond in accordance with our intentions and values.

Knowing ourselves means understanding our physical, mental and emotional abilities and limitations. An unsafe situation for me may be safe for someone else or vice versa.

Assessment of others is an essential aspect of self-defense. The critical parts are to determine how committed the person is to being respectful of others and what their level of self-control is. Recognize that both of these vary with mood, intoxication and external events.

Consequently, it is best to make a general assessment of a person, and also an assessment of how they are doing in the moment. Assessment like this takes time, because you need to be able to observe the person in a variety of situations and when relaxed or in stress.

Examples:
- John is respectful of women's sexual boundaries when sober but inappropriate when drunk. His self-control diminishes with intoxication as does his commitment to treating women with respect.

- Jane is generally kind and considerate, but when she gets angry the gloves come off and she becomes verbally abusive. Her commitment to respect for others deteriorates with increases in self-protectiveness and anger. Her self-control decreases with her physiological arousal.

It is also essential to assess yourself in the same way. The primary "opponent" in martial arts (and any other kind of personal development) is ourselves. Character is created over the long term through wise choices and developing good habits. We must all struggle with our own challenges with selfishness, laziness, impatience, and self-discipline (to name a few!). Hopefully, as we age we will also mature, developing greater self-control and a deeper commitment to respecting others.

Examples of habitual, unconscious disrespect:

- Jack wonders why people seem to keep him at a distance. He does not consider that his habit of criticizing others might have something to do with it.

- As a young girl, Sally learned to get her way with her parents by complaining. As an adult, this has evolved into a habitually whiney tone of voice. This puts many people off.

Assailants vary in terms of selfishness and in terms of self-control. People who are habitually selfish and often out of control are much more likely to perpetrate violence against others. Assessing these factors accurately will allow you to make better predictions about the behavior of others (and of yourself as well). Let's look more closely at the range of respect and selfishness we are likely to encounter.

Unusually respectful family, friends and associates value kindness and have developed habits of generosity and caring. Their commitment to compassion manifests in their everyday relationships. They treat those with less power (children and animals) gently. Most people like this have a spiritual inspiration for their commitment to respecting others. Personally, I aspire to becoming ever more compassionate and kind. How about you?

Normally self-absorbed family, friends and associates pay less attention to the needs and preferences of others and do not have an unusual commitment to treating others with respect and compassion. They will generally behave in a way that is socially acceptable, but this may come from a fear of negative consequences, not necessarily a genuine caring for others. They have not placed a high value on kindness and compassion, nor purposefully studied and practiced these behaviors as skills. This manifests in their everyday relationships. Their verbal and non-verbal behavior can be harsh, judgemental and blaming. Their behavior towards themselves and to those with less power can be bullying and coercive. Many people act this way habitually, unconsciously, and out of ignorance, with no actual intent to harm. Unfortunately the lack of intent does not make what they do less harmful.

This leaves the extreme category of assailant – **the criminally selfish.** These are abnormally selfish family, friends and associates. Like everyone else, they look for opportunities and means to fulfill their needs and desires, but with little to no concern for how their behavior impacts others. They lie. They prioritize what they want much more highly than what anyone else wants. They can act in societally acceptable ways if it helps them achieve their goals. On their best days they look normally self-absorbed. Their relationships are power, dominance and control based. They tend to treat themselves and others harshly. Some criminally selfish individuals practice being charming and looking kind in order to manipulate their victims. Many abusers, addicts and alcoholics act this selfishly.

In our assessment of others, we start with evaluating their commitment to being respectful of others. As we have seen, individuals vary in terms of selfishness, and this trait can change slowly over time for better or worse. Individuals also vary in terms of self-control, but this can change in seconds. A person can seem in control one moment and can be losing it in another. To understand this, we need to understand the primary factors which undermine self-control.

Factors influencing self-control:

There are four primary factors which undermine self-control. These are stress, emotional distress, sexual arousal and intoxication.

- Stress includes specific events of an ordinary bad day as well as longer term stressors of financial hardship, or mental or physical illness. It is also strongly impacted by biological factors such as blood sugar, sleep, exercise and social contact. Stress shortens a person's fuse.

- Emotional distress can be due to something in the present, a reminder of past pain, or a worry about the future. The primary distressing emotions are anger, sadness, fear and shame.

- During sexual arousal, blood leaves the frontal cortex and goes to the genitals. Thinking, planning and delaying gratification is not as easy. Young adults are less experienced handling sexual arousal and can have a particularly difficult time delaying gratification.

- Intoxication, whether from alcohol or drugs, can reduce inhibitions. Drunken or stoned people often do things they would not do when sober, and then later regret them.

Each of these four factors may be large or non-existent for a given person at any given time. Their effect in terms of reducing self-control is cumulative.

For example, normally selfish people can act criminally selfish:

- Peter is worried about losing his job due to corporate downsizing. Fretting about this, he stops at a bar for a couple of drinks. As he drinks, he dwells on the injustices he has suffered in his work life, and how this is only the latest version. He leaves the bar fuming. At home his wife asks him about his day. Although Peter would normally have understood this as a gesture of caring, under these circumstances he hears it as yet another example of the world not understanding him. He yells at his wife, which leads to a horrible fight that gets physical.

- Frank takes Jean out on a date and they go drinking and dancing. Later, Jean is less inhibited than usual and more physically affectionate. Frank becomes more sexual, which Jean welcomes to a point and then starts to say, "No". Frank's self-control is reduced by his intoxication and his sexual arousal. He is frustrated with her and rationalizes that since he paid for her dinner and drinks she "owes" him sex. He forces himself on her.

Most frequently, this kind of abuse of women is part of a pattern of criminally selfish power and control.

Complete self-defense includes not only doing what you can to not be victimized, it also entails doing what you can to make sure that you do not perpetrate.

If I am stressed, upset, aroused and intoxicated, I will not be thinking clearly and will likely make some poor choices. Preferring not to do this, I protect myself from these risk factors. Despite my best efforts, however, I am still prone to speaking harshly to my children when, for example, they do not cooperate with my agenda for them to tidy up and go to bed after I've had a long day.

By assessing myself constantly for my current level of self-control, I can take steps to cool down or absent myself before I am tested. There are some nights where everything goes better if I just ask my wife to put the kids to bed! This is a version of "not being at the point of conflict".

We can help ourselves and others be more in control by managing these four risk factors; stress, emotional upset, sexual arousal and intoxication.

Stress: Wise stress management can include quality diet, sleep, exercise (T'ai Chi!), relaxation and applied spirituality (such as meditation or prayer). I can manage my own stress by keeping myself on track with these. I can help my family, friends and associates by encouraging them to do the same. When I notice myself or others getting more stressed, I can point this out and support them taking care of themselves.

Emotional Upset: Some emotional upset is rooted in the past, or based on worries of the future, and some is responsive to the present. Clearing out emotional baggage from the past lengthens our fuse for the present. If I see myself or my family, friends or associates carrying a lot of past baggage, or trapped in depression or anxiety, I can encourage them to seek counseling. If I see myself or my family, friends or associates upset about the present, this is an opportunity for me to practice my skills in compassion and kindness to offer some kind of soothing contact.

Sexual Arousal: Not to be crass, but by recognizing that sexual arousal impacts self-control, we can take responsibility for our own levels of arousal. Sexual release with a partner or through masturbation can quickly restore self-control.

Most reported rapes occur on dates (57%). There seem to be two kinds of perpetrators: the majority are criminally selfish, men who plot to rape as an expression of anger and the desire to have "power over". Many of these men are repeat offenders and are thus responsible for the vast majority of rapes. For these men, rape is consistent with their values. (For further information about rape and rapists, see the work of Dr. David Lisak summarized here: www.sexualassault.army.mil/files/RAPE_FACT_SHEET.pdf).

There are also some date rapists that have the ignorant attitude that they have the right to expect sex after spending time and money on a date. This is the kind of behavior that (if you are a man), you need to protect yourself from perpetrating. As a woman, careful interviewing may reveal this kind of ignorance.

Intoxication: Many people enjoy drinking and using other substances to help them relax and socialize. If you do this or spend time with others who do, recognize this as the risk factor it is for loss of control. Knowing that intoxication impairs judgement and impulse control, I can remain clean and sober or practice moderation in my use of substances. I can avoid being in places where people are predictably intoxicated, and I can choose friends and associates who are sober or moderate in their own use. If I see family, friends or associates becoming intoxicated, I may choose to distance myself from them for the time being. If this is chronic, I may try to intervene or habitually avoid them.

Creating safe, respectful relationships:

Understanding selfishness and the four factors influencing self-control, gives us more tools for assessing ourselves and others effectively and thus creating safe and respectful relationships.

My first task is to polish my own character and become "unusually respectful". I can work to change my offensive habits and to practice compassion and respect for others as behavioral skills. Using my awareness skills, I can work to not offend or frighten others to the point that they attack me or run from me. If I do offend someone, I can choose to repair the relationship rather than becoming self-protective and belligerent myself.

Turning our attention to others, many people already identify some members of their social circle as selfish and/or having poor self-control. You may find others as you assess people more purposefully. You might find yourself trapped in a relationship with a person (eg: sibling, parent, coworker) who acts selfishly or has very limited self-control. If they are not responsive to efforts to influence them, the most effective self-defense is usually avoidance. Most of us, at some time in our lives, have had to keep our distance from someone who easily became verbally or physically disrespectful or abusive. Avoidance includes maintaining physical space from the person as well as protecting yourself from verbal interactions.

Unfortunately, in some cases, avoiding this person (eg: an alcoholic parent) may be impossible. Even if you can, often avoidance is not fully satisfactory in that it does not necessarily end the conflict. However, if the source of the conflict is the other person's poor habits, truly ending the conflict requires the other person to change. Although you can make requests for change, ultimately this is out of your control, so doing your best at avoidance may be your best option.

A very important aspect of self-defense here is to make sure that you can honestly hold yourself blameless for the recurrent conflict. Avoidance doesn't work if you still purposefully, unknowingly or "unconsciously" push the other person's buttons.

As you become more skilled, you become able to almost completely manage the risk of attacking or being attacked by normal family, friends and associates. At this point in my own life, I have built resilient habits around respect for others and self-control and am able to assess others pretty accurately for where they are in these terms at any given time. I can also set limits that maintain physical and emotional distance between me and those who are acting selfish or out of control. In addition, I continue to practice my skills and habits of compassion and respect for others and myself. Hopefully, you are already building your skills in these ways also.

Unfortunately, you will never be able to fully protect yourself from the **criminally selfish,** the same way that you can never fully protect yourself from lightning and meteorites. Fortunately, just like meteorites, the criminally selfish are unusual. Once again, our awareness skills can help us manage the risk these individuals pose. If we are fortunate, we can prevent having to deal with this kind of assault.

Understanding that the person in this frame of mind is simply waiting for opportunities and means to perpetrate, we must be equally alert to avoiding them. Remember that this attacker may be a stranger or someone "known" whom you have improperly assessed or who has lost control. In either case, manage your risk by preventing means and opportunities for people to hurt you.

Here are two examples of what can happen if steps are not taken to prevent potential perpetrators from having means or opportunities. This kind of behavior may arise from the naïve denial of the existence of the criminally selfish and of how hurtful their trespass can be. Some people may actually pride themselves on acting as if criminals do not exist – unfortunately, acting as if rattlesnakes and black widows do not exist is not an effective way to stay safe.

Example:
- Ken feels safe living in a small town with friendly neighbors and never locks his door. One evening he returns home to find his kitchen trashed, his clothes and furniture destroyed, and his electronic equipment stolen. Not only has he lost his goods, but he feels violated and bitter.

In this case Ken did not maintain control of means (the unlocked door) and opportunity (him being away from home). This left him vulnerable.

- Sally, who lives alone, answers her door to find Paul, an associate. Sally does not know Paul well, but when he asks if he can use the phone due to car trouble, she lets him in despite her misgivings. Once inside, Paul assaults her.

In this case, Sally didn't have enough information to adequately assess Paul and followed social norms rather than listening to her misgivings.

It behooves us to consider how a criminal might violate us and take steps to make it more difficult. This includes locking houses, apartments and cars, and controlling with whom we are alone. Listen to your intuition – it is information about something that you simply have not yet been able to verbalize. Pay particular attention if there are times when you feel more vulnerable or more likely to be victimized.

Since criminals are looking for easy ways to meet their selfish desires, we want to make it clear that we are not easy marks. We convey this through assertive, self-confident movement and posture, and the willingness to speak and act forcefully when uncomfortable. Sometimes the discomfort will be a subtle cue from your intuition. Take these seriously! It is far better to protect yourself unnecessarily than to look back and wish you had.

Be alert for opportunities for attack created by darkness, solitude and transitions like unlocking cars or doors. Specific practices may include avoiding dark areas, carefully checking nooks in parking garages, having your keys ready on approaching your car, being prepared to verbally warn off someone who is getting too close and many others. Other parking garage tips include being aware of the car parked beside your driver's door as you approach – check for occupants and be especially cautious if that car is a van. Never get into a car with an attacker. Whatever they mean to do to you will be easier once they have you in a location of their choosing. Fight to the death before you get in the car.

There is value in doing reading or taking training on this topic to help you manage opportunity and means more effectively and thereby avoid being at the point of conflict. I encourage you to take your own safety seriously and prepare to not be victimized.

These tips are for protecting yourself from strangers. As you will recall, although men are a bit more likely to be assaulted by strangers, women are statistically more likely to know the assailant. Keeping this in mind, practice asking yourself about your assessment of different people. Be sensitive to your intuition or gut feeling and assume that it is correct. Play with asking people questions such as, "Tell me about a time when you got really angry – what did you do?" Or try, "What would it take for you to yell and call me names? Under what circumstances might you hit me?" This can give you important new information, both in terms of the content of the answer and the self-comfort and self-knowledge it displays. Recognize that the criminally selfish will lie, and may be quite charming about it. Trust your gut and your intuition. Expect assessment to take some time and allow yourself to require others to earn your trust.

Physical Self-Defense

By now it should be clear how the basic rules of self-defense, "Know Yourself And Your Opponent" and "Don't Be At The Point Of Conflict", are first applied to avoid the situations that give rise to an attack in the first place. Practice your skills and awareness including paying attention to your intuition. Unfortunately, even a master may find him or herself simply in the wrong place at the wrong time, or being targeted on the basis of race, gender, sexual preference etc.

Let's first categorize attacks in terms of the appropriate response. By appropriate, I mean the level of deterrence required to stop the attack. In responding to an attack, start mellow and be prepared to escalate instantly if the attack continues. First, make the perpetrator do more work to reach you (run!) and point out unpleasant long-term consequences. If they persist, make them endure more pain in order to reach you (strike out). If they persist, cause them lasting physical damage or death (go for their eyes and throat).

We can also look at physical attacks in terms of the intent of the perpetrator. He thinks attacking you is an effective way to get what he wants. If you understand what that is, you will be more effective in defending yourself. The following three types of attack are listed in order of descending likelihood.

A personal angry attack. Here the perpetrator feels hurt, wronged and self-righteously angry at you. He thinks that hurting you will make him safer and is the best way to make his pain stop.

In the best case with this kind of an attack, if you let the person vent his anger without causing him more pain, he will naturally regain control and settle to a calmer place. Because of this, it is best to avoid this kind of attack while allowing your opponent to use up his energy. If you can, simply run away. If you are trapped and must be physical, continue to try to avoid the attack. Deflect and counter if necessary to stay safe, but recognize that if you cause him pain or make him fearful, this can contribute to the attacker's self-righteous anger. Use your words to convey concern, understanding and calm. Also point out long-term negative consequences of the attack.

Ex: Jim's angry neighbor takes a swing at him. While avoiding the swing, Jim moves away to a safer distance saying, "Hey, Charlie, I get that you are really angry with me. I want to understand what's going on for you. Can't we just talk about this? I figure we're going to be neighbors for awhile and I would really like to get along."

An attack designed to control you in order to take something from you. Muggings and robberies are of this type. The perpetrator thinks that by attacking you he can get the goods or experience he wants. The perpetrator is acting from a criminally selfish mindset. Often perpetrators of this kind of attack use a weapon or the threat of violence to ensure rapid compliance. Sometimes these attacks can lead to deadly violence.

We control means and opportunity first by exercising care around displaying the goods that a selfish person might want to steal. We have learned not to flash wads of hundreds in seedy bars.

When you have goods that someone might want to steal, don't put yourself in a position that might give a lurking criminal an edge. A greater level of alertness is required. For instance, as a traveler, I have learned that taking an expensive camera to the beach does not make for a relaxing day.

A related class of attack is the Targeted Population Attack. Here the attacker is trying to physically harm or humiliate you as a member of a targeted group. They are not angry at you personally, nor are they trying to take your goods, instead, they are attacking you as a member of a targeted group. These attacks are based on gender, race, religion, sexual preference, social class and many others. Each of us is vulnerable to this kind of attack, if in the wrong place. Unfortunately, some people are not able to avoid being subject to this kind of prejudice and vulnerability. This is a social problem, and, sadly, until it is solved at this level, "minorities" will always have to be more careful.

For instance, women need to have a greater level of alertness whenever they feel that the opportunity for an attack may exist. They should also recognize the potential edge in terms of means that scarves or high heels might provide an attacker.

In some cases it is possible to disguise or simply not display your group affiliation and thus avoid the negative attention you might otherwise receive. Examples of this include "don't ask, don't tell" strategies and actual disguise.

Some targeted population attacks are at the level of verbal harassment. At other times the intent is to hurt, rape or kill. As with the attack targeting your goods, it is best to start by responding as if the attack is of a lesser intensity while being ready to instantly accelerate if necessary.

In the best case with this kind of an attack, as you make the perpetrator work hard to reach you (run away!) or demonstrate that it will be painful for him to persist in his attack (threaten his eyes, throat, or groin), or that he is likely to be caught (yell, "Fire!"), he will give up and look for an easier mark.

Please note: Training to be able to do this when faced with a weapon is beyond the typical martial arts hobbyist. If the attacker has the benefits of surprise and superior size or strength (which he will try to do) you may well not be able to bring your physical self-defense abilities to bear effectively.

Some martial arts training may not actually improve your self-defense skills as much as you might expect due to the limitations placed on training for the safety of the participants. Even boxing, wrestling and cage fighting have safety based limitations on attacks. Many of the most effective defensive responses, such as counters to the eyes, neck and groin, are too dangerous to practice on an unprotected opponent. The best training is an accurate simulation of an actual assault with full contact defense. "Model Mugging" type programs are very helpful because the "muggers" wear full protective gear so that defenders can respond without needing to worry about hurting them.

An important aspect of self-defense is being prepared to survive an assault with your physical and mental health intact. For the physical part, this means being prepared to give the person what he wants rather than risking permanent injury or death. You know the old joke:
Hood with a gun: "Your money or your life!"
W.C. Fields: Pause
"Come on Pops, your money or your life!"
W.C. Fields: "I'm thinking, I'm thinking!"

This is a particularly horrible thing to have to think about in terms of sexual assault, but self-defense is all about preparing physically and mentally for the worst case scenario. So please, seriously consider under what circumstances you would choose to not fight back against a sexual assault. The clarity brought by forethought will increase your resourcefulness if this should ever happen to you.

In terms of our mental resilience, research is clear that survivors of traumatic attacks are more likely to weather them without developing debilitating PTSD (Post Traumatic Stress Disorder) when they
1. are able to stay alert and present during the attack
2. can integrate these attacks into their existing world view
3. have good social support after the attack

Martial arts training (and other preparation) can be very helpful with these in terms of:

1. Practicing keeping your eyes open and breathing during frightening drills

2. Developing a realistic view of the world that includes the reality of the criminally selfish and situations that may require you to fight for your life

3. Building relationships with others who share your understanding of the world so that if necessary they can help you through the recovery process from an attack

The fourth and rarest attack is one designed to kill you. This is the most difficult kind of attack to protect yourself from, and, fortunately, the least likely to happen if you practice self-defense basics and are not in the armed services or the protective services. Assuming that you are maintaining peaceful enough relationships with your family, friends and associates, a murderous assailant will be a crazed associate or stranger, a criminally minded assassin, or a terrorist. The attacker will almost certainly have a weapon.

For most of us, developing realistic self-defense skills against an attacker with an assault rifle is simply not worth the effort given how unlikely such an attack is. As I mentioned above, effective defense against a weapon, even a knife, is beyond most recreational martial artists.

Should you have the misfortune of being in this situation and you have the opportunity to counter, do so ruthlessly. Aim to do permanent or deadly damage to your opponent as quickly as possible. Know that you have the moral high ground in that he has initiated this battle, not you.

In some cases such as flight # 93, it may make sense to suffer severe injury or death to protect others. Only take this course if sure that you will be effective at stopping the threat. It will not help your kids if you get yourself killed trying to protect them and the attacker is still able to harm them.

In closing, let's review the key points of this appendix:

The highest level of self-defense is preventing violence and preserving life. Assess yourself and others honestly and correctly in terms of 1) respect for others and 2) self-control. Respect the four factors that undermine self-control. Limit the opportunity and means others have to hurt you in order to preserve your safety. Do not be at the point of conflict. If you find yourself there, avoid first, deflect second and only counter when necessary.

Assailants vary in terms of selfishness and self-control. For simplicity, we discussed three types of assailants: 1) normal family, friends and associates who are expressing passing aggression 2) selfish family, friends and associates with poor self-control 3) the criminally selfish.

Self-control is compromised by stress, emotional distress, sexual arousal, and intoxication. Manage these factors in yourself and monitor them in others.

Attacks vary in terms of viciousness and commitment. We discussed four types of attacks ranging from the more common to the rare 1) personal angry attacks 2) attacks designed to control you and take something from you 3) targeted population attacks and 4) attacks designed to kill you.

Self-defense has three stages: preparing for and avoiding danger, dealing with the attack, and processing the after-affects. Reading this appendix is a good step in preparing for and avoiding violence. The next step is building the skills required to assess yourself and others for selfishness and self-control. Also develop and hone your skills in managing means and opportunity so that you are not an easy target. Pay attention to your intuition as a source of subtle, not yet verbalized, information. Work on your physical self-defense skills in a realistic way that hones your awareness and that physically favors targets such as eyes, throat, and groin. Finally, prepare to survive any attack by adjusting your world view to include the criminally selfish and by building a social network that would be able to comfort you following an attack.

May this discussion help you stay safe.

A good book for further reading is:

The Gift of Fear by Gavin de Becker, Dell, 1997

Bibliography:

Babin, Michael – <u>T'ai Chi Chuan; The Martial Side</u>, Paladin Press, Boulder, CO, 1992 This book is a valuable discussion of a variety of topics of value to those interested in the martial art of T'ai Chi.

Chia, Mantak has written a number of excellent books mostly on qigong and energy cultivation. Here are some titles: <u>Awakening Healing Energy Through The Tao</u>, <u>Iron Shirt Chi Kung</u>, Healing Tao Publisher, Huntington, NY.

Chuckrow, Robert – <u>The Tai Chi Book</u>, YMAA, Boston MA, 1998 A readable overview with clear suggestions on refining your practice in the Cheng Man Ch-ing tradition.

Crompton, Paul – <u>T'ai Chi for Two</u>, Shambala, 1989. This is a good introduction to simple push hands and he also includes a number of drills for specific movements from the form.
<u>T'ai Chi Combat,</u> Shambala, 1999. This is a valuable discussion of applying T'ai Chi to combat including an effort to put complex terms and descriptions into simple English. He presents a number of drills and a simple San Shou form.

Jou, Tsung Hwa – <u>The Tao of Tai–Chi Chuan</u>, The Tai Chi Foundation, Warwick, NY, 1988 - A readable textbook on T'ai Chi.

Kauz, Herman – <u>Push-Hands</u>, Overlook Press, Woodstock, NY, 1997 Mr. Kauz, a student of CMC, writes an introductory section that goes into his views on competition and the importance of practicing a non-competitive attitude in Push Hands and investing in loss. The next section is on a simple two handed pattern for push hands and pointers for how to use the drill to best benefit. He includes some great tips. It is an easy read and you are sure to pick up some valuable ideas. I whole heartedly agree with the points he raises about competition and recommend this book to my students for this section as well as for his practical tips.

Klein, Bob – <u>Movements of Magic</u>, Newcastle, North Hollywood, CA, 1984
<u>Movements of Power</u>, Newcastle, 1990

Loupos, John – <u>Inside Tai Chi</u>, YMAA, Boston, MA, 2002
<u>Exploring Tai Chi</u>, YMAA, Boston, MA, 2003
These are both quite readable and valuable books that touch on issues relevant to push hands from a Yang style perspective.

Ma, Yueh-liang & Zee, Wen – <u>Wu Style Taichichuan Push-Hands</u>, Shanghai Book Co. 1995. An overview of the subject that suffers a bit from translation. Some of the descriptions are hard to follow.

Olson, Stuart Alve, has translated and authored a number of useful books. Here are two. Trans. – <u>T'ai Chi Sensing Hands</u>, Multi Media Books, 1999 – A very thorough, careful, and advanced examination of push hands written by Chen Kung. I find the written descriptions of movements quite challenging to follow.

Trans. – <u>The Intrinsic Energies of T'ai Chi Chuan</u>, Dragon Door, St Paul MN, 1994.

Ralston, Peter – <u>Cheng Hsin T'ui Shou: The Art of Effortless Power</u>, North Atlantic Books, Berkeley, 1991. An excellent overview of a large number of techniques presented in clear language from a depth of understanding. Ralston is more concerned with effective movement than with traditional forms.

Russell, Jonathan – <u>The T'ai Chi Two-Person Dance</u>, North Atlantic Books, Berkeley, CA, 2004. This is a presentation of T.T. Liang's San Shou form in which he has integrated push hands and Da Lu. Mr. Russell's introductory chapters are clear, readable and quite useful for push hands.

Sigman, Mike – his material is on the web at <u>http://www.iay.org.uk/internal-strength/</u> I highly recommend it.

Wong, Kiew Kit – <u>The Complete Book of T'ai Chi Chuan</u>, Element, Rockport MA, 1996 – This book includes some interesting moving step variations and martial application patterns.

Yang, Jwing-Ming is a clear and prolific writer. His books are excellent. Here are some titles : –<u>Yang Style T'ai Chi Chuan</u>, <u>Advanced</u> <u>Yang Style T'ai Chi Chuan Vol 1 & 2</u>, <u>The Essence of Tai Chi Chi Kung</u>, <u>Shaolin Chin Na</u>, He also has a video/DVD series on Push Hands. YMAA Publication Center, Jamaica Plain, MA.

Check the T'ai Chi Magazine catalogue or website (<u>www.tai-chi.com</u>) for a selection of videos and DVDs on Push Hands

On the web:

Visit my site for free articles and updates: http://www.nando-r.com

Search <u>http://www.egreenway.com/taichichuan/index.htm</u> for a vast number of links

Visit <u>http://www.gilmanstudio.com/</u> for free articles and lessons thanks to Michael Gilman

Visit <u>http://www.taijiworld.com/</u> for free articles and lessons thanks to Erle Montaigue. He also has a number of interesting books exploring Dim Mak or the striking of vital points in self defense.

Made in the USA
Lexington, KY
19 June 2013